Polly Pinder's
Chocolate Cookbook

Polly Pinder's Chocolate Cookbook

First published 1988
Search Press Ltd.,
Wellwood, North Farm Road,
Tunbridge Wells, Kent TN2 3DR

This book specially produced for The Leisure Circle
by Search Press.

Photographs by Search Press Studios
Drawings by Polly Pinder

Typeset by Pentacor Ltd., High Wycombe, Bucks
Printed in Hong Kong by Everbest Printing Co., Ltd.

CONTENTS

Cakes Buns & Slices
PAGE 69

Biscuits & Bars
PAGE 83

Hot Puddings
PAGE 97

Cold Desserts

Sauces

Drinks

Index

Introduction

Why do so many of us have a passion, a yearning for chocolate? Why does this rich, smooth, semi-sweet substance offer such sensuous delight? The reason always seems to elude me but, in these days of gastronomic sophistication, when so many luscious foods are regarded as unhealthy (not that I necessarily disagree), it almost seems as if the natural perversity in human beings leads us all the more towards such forbidden fruit.

Chocolate is the treat, the reward, the gold-wrapped gift and, for me, especially when accompanied by freshly made coffee, the crowning of a perfect meal. This book is a tribute to chocolate's amazing versatility: its ability to transform the most ordinary of sweet dishes and to enhance the most delicious. It also seems to me that chocolate, as a medium for design in the culinary arts, has a potential which has not yet been exploited. A whole new world of chocolate awaits us.

The early part of the book is concerned with the traditional methods of using and treating chocolate – the making and decorating of confectionery, and the wonderful chocolate creations for those extra-special occasions one can make, including delights like 'Swan Lake', the chocolate box, the bird cage and the geranium tree. These are not as difficult to make as they first appear. The latter part of the book offers recipes for delicious cakes, biscuits and bars; hot and cold puddings; and sauces and drinks, all playing variations on the chocolate theme. As with my previous books on decorating cakes, I have come to the subject of chocolate knowing only how to eat it. It is not years of skill and training that one needs, however, just time, patience, the strength of mind to resist the temptation of satin-smooth melted chocolate, and the ability to follow easy step-by-step instructions.

The Origins and Development of Chocolate

Cocoa powder and the many different types of chocolate – plain, milk, white, cooking, couveture – are all derived from cocoa beans, which are the seeds of the fruit of the cacao tree. These small trees are native to tropical America but are extensively cultivated elsewhere in the tropics. They can only be profitably cultivated within 20° north or south of the equator, and they need a rich porous soil of considerable depth, evenly distributed rainfall, and protection from the wind.

The tree begins to bear fruit when it is four or five years old. The small pink flowers and succeeding fruit pods grow directly from the trunk and main branches. On average a full-grown tree may produce 6,000 flowers, only twenty of which will become pods. A pod weighs about 450g (1lb) and contains 20–40 seeds, or cocoa beans, which resemble plump almonds and are covered with a sweet white pulp. The skin of the bean is brown and the flesh of the superior type is of a

cinnamon colour. The ordinary bean has dark brown or purple flesh and the poorer type is the colour of slate. The flavour of the bean is rather bitter and astringent, nutty, and faintly aromatic.

The Mayas and the Aztecs of Central America, or what is now Mexico, were the first known drinkers of chocolate. In 1519 the Spanish explorer Cortes discovered the beverage and, after observing that the Aztec Emperor, Montezuma, drank copious amounts daily (no doubt using it as a stimulant), he introduced it to the Spanish Court. The drinking chocolate was made by drying the cocoa beans and roasting them over a fire. Water was then added and the beans were pounded to a paste. Often spices, nuts and powdered flowers were added.

Cocoa was introduced into England during the seventeenth century and for many years was an expensive luxury, high prices being sustained by heavy import duties. In 1835 Gladstone lowered the duty on 450g (1lb) of cocoa beans to one penny.

Whilst Joseph Fry was the first Englishman to produce eating chocolate, it was a Dutchman, Coenraad van Houten who, several years before, had invented a press which could extract cocoa butter from the bean.

The chocolate-making process is somewhat long and involved. When the seeds (cocoa beans) have been scooped from the pods, they are piled on to leaves, covered with more leaves and left for several days. The sugary pulp surrounding the beans first begins to ferment, then it slowly drains away as the temperature rises. From time to time the beans are turned to give an even fermentation. In some countries the beans are fermented in boxes and poured from one to another each day.

After fermentation the wet beans are laid on coconut mats or wooden platforms to dry in the sun. Again they are turned at regular intervals. In certain areas the climate is such that artificial dryers must be used. When the drying is complete, the beans are packed into bags and stored in warehouses ready for transportation.

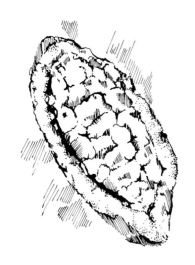

At their factory destination the beans are sorted, cleaned and roasted for an hour in revolving drums. The temperature for roasting is lower than that for coffee, about 275°F or 135°C.

The roasted beans are then 'kibbled', a process in which they pass between rolls of serrated cones placed at such a distance apart that the beans are cracked rather than crushed. The cracked shell is carried off by an air blast: this is called 'winnowing'. The broken beans or 'nibs' are ground between steel rollers. Because the cocoa beans are 50% fat (cocoa butter) and the grinding process generates heat, the crisp nutty cocoa nibs emerge as thick brown fluid. When cooled this solidifies to a hard block of unsweetened chocolate known as 'mass'. This is the basis of all chocolate products.

Cocoa is made by extracting 70%–80% of the butter. The hard dry cake which remains is then ground, re-ground, and sieved through fine mesh.

To make plain chocolate, extra cocoa butter and powdered sugar are added to the 'mass'. Milk chocolate has sweetened full cream milk added which has been condensed into a rich creamy liquid. At these stages the chocolate has a rough texture. After being ground and mixed (pummelled) the liquid chocolate is 'conched' by heavy rollers to produce a smooth velvety texture. The chocolate is now ready to be moulded into bars. In order to make it more malleable, more cocoa butter is added for confectionery and coated biscuits.

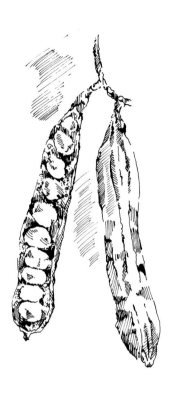

Carob

For anyone who prefers to use a naturally sweet alternative to chocolate, a carob confectionery is ideal. This comes in bar form similar to chocolate, and it contains important vitamins and minerals. It is also free from caffeine. It can be melted like chocolate and has a rich, smooth texture. Carob powder can also be used as a substitute for cocoa; it gives a different but very good rich flavour to cakes, desserts and biscuits.

The carob-tree is widely diffused, spontaneously and by cultivation, from Spain to the eastern Mediterranean regions. It can take fifteen years before fruit is produced regularly and twenty years before the tree reaches its full height of 40–50 feet, or 12–15 metres. Male, female and hermaphrodite flowers blossom during September and October, with the occasional winter flowering if the season is particularly mild.

The seed pods can be 4–10 inches, or 100–250 millimetres, in length. At first they seem to resemble green broad beans, but with maturity the leathery pods turn dark brown and the surface becomes glossy. Each pod contains up to 15 seeds with sweet pulpy division between them.

When the pods ripen, they fall naturally from the trees and are harvested between September and November. They are first cleaned, then broken roughly to separate the pulp from the seeds. They are processed to make a gum which is used in edible products as an emulsifier or stabilising agent.

The pods are roasted, milled, and sieved to form a fine powder. This is ready to use in home-baking or commercial food manufacture. Carob confectionery, usually produced in bars, is made by adding raw sugar cane, vegetable fats, and skimmed milk to the powder.

Cooking with Chocolate

Cooking with Chocolate

I have used cocoa and dessert chocolate for all the recipes in this book. Carob powder and carob confectionery can be substituted in all cases apart from those in the section, 'Chocolate Creations', where the variation in colour can only be achieved by using and mixing plain, milk and white chocolate.

Cooking chocolate or cake covering cannot be considered a true chocolate because some of the cocoa butter has been replaced by vegetable oils. It is cheaper than dessert chocolate and easy to melt and use, but the flavour, in my opinion, is poor in comparison.

Couveture is a special confectioners' chocolate with a high proportion of cocoa butter. It has a rich glossy finish and brittle texture, but it is not as easy to work with as dessert chocolate. It is also rather expensive and sometimes difficult to obtain.

Cocoa

As the flavour of cocoa is fairly strong, it is unwise to be over-generous with it when baking cakes and biscuits. Although it is thoroughly sieved before packing, another sifting, along with other dry ingredients, is always to be recommended.

When making chocolate butter icing, for example, the cocoa should first be blended to a smooth paste with drops of very hot, but not boiling, water. This will cook the starch in the cocoa.

Melting Chocolate

When melting chocolate, there are two important points for you to remember. First, do not allow steam or water to get into the chocolate. Second, do not burn it.

Break the chocolate into pieces, place these in a double saucepan, or a basin which fits snugly into a pan. The water should not touch the bottom of the basin. Bring the water to boil first, remove it from the heat, then place the basin or pan over and leave the chocolate to melt. Before you use the chocolate, stir it to a smooth creamy consistency. It will remain fluid for some time.

Dipping Chocolate

In order to make the chocolate more fluid when dipping confectionery or pieces of fresh fruit, vegetable oil can be added. Use one tablespoon (tblsp) or half an ounce (15g) of solid vegetable oil to every 6oz (170g) of chocolate. Special two- or three-pronged dipping forks are available at good kitchen supply shops. When I first bought one I did not find it very useful until I bent it to an angle of 90°.

To dip the confectionery or fruit, place it on the fork (an ordinary dinner fork will suffice but, again, it is easier to use if the handle has been bent) and lower it into the melted chocolate. Carefully lift it, then scrape off any excess chocolate on the sides of the basin. With the help of a skewer, push the confectionery carefully on to a sheet of waxed or non-stick silicone paper. Leave the chocolates to set in a cool room, unless stated otherwise in the recipe.

Grating Chocolate

Grating is easier if the chocolate has first been chilled in the refrigerator for about 30 minutes. Wrap a piece of double kitchen towel around the lower half of the chocolate bar, as this will delay any melting from warm hands.

Piping Chocolate

When piping chocolate, lift the basin or top of the double saucepan away from the boiled water and leave it to cool for 5–10 minutes before using. This will make the chocolate less runny and easier to control.

Snipping the point from an icing bag is adequate for some piping, but for more refined decorative work better results are achieved by using plain tube icing nozzles 1, 2 or 3.

As with most decorating skills, a little practice on waxed or silicone paper will give you confidence and familiarise you with the new medium. Use sheets of greaseproof paper to make the icing bags (see diagram). All practice work can be re-melted and used again.

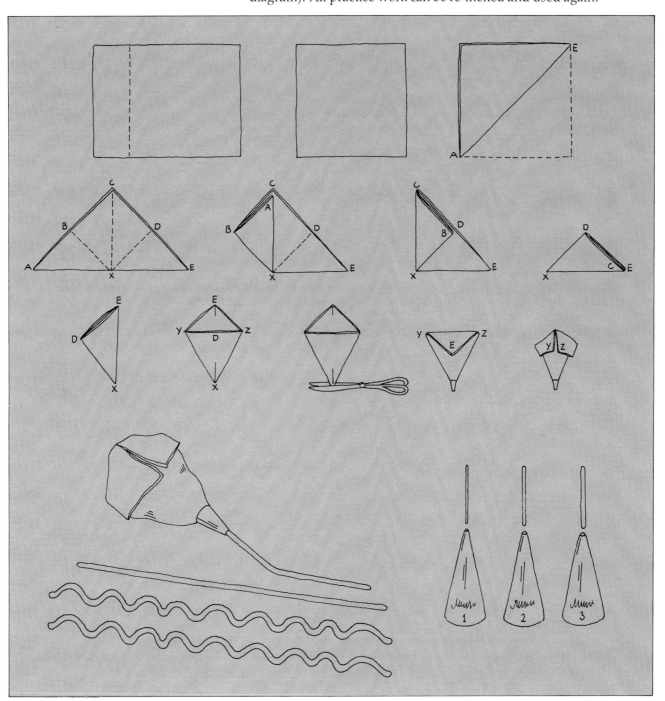

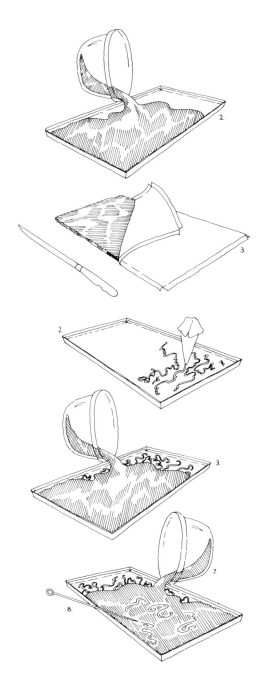

Cutting Shapes

Shapes can be cut to your own design, using a sharp-pointed knife and a cardboard template. You can also use biscuit cutters or cocktail cutters. The quantity of chocolate needed will depend on how many shapes you require – better to have too much rather than too little, to allow for practising and the odd mistake. Any leftovers, broken pieces and mis-shapes can be remelted and used at a later date.

1. Line a scrupulously cleaned baking tray with greaseproof, waxed or silicone paper.
2. Melt the chocolate as described on page 15. Pour it into the tin and leave it to set in a cool room. The thickness of the chocolate can vary from between 2mm to 5mm (1⁄16in. to 5⁄32in.).
3. Carefully turn the chocolate on to a marble slab or formica chopping board. Peel away the lining paper.
4. The chocolate is now ready for cutting. Try to handle it as little as possible.

Random two-toned pattern effects can be achieved in two ways and with varying combinations of plain, milk and white chocolate. For a definite pattern:
1. Melt some white chocolate and put 2–3 tablespoonsful in an icing bag.
2. Snip the end off the bag, then drizzle the chocolate (make squiggly lines) on the surface of the lined baking tin.
3. Leave the chocolate to set.
4. Meanwhile, melt some plain or milk chocolate, or both, separately.
5. Leave the chocolate to cool slightly, then pour it over the white chocolate. Leave to set.
6. Carefully turn on to marble or formica and peel away the lining paper. The chocolate is now ready for cutting.
For a random marble effect:
7. Follow steps 1 and 2 above (using different combinations of chocolate if wished), then add the melted main-colour immediately.
8. Using a skewer, swirl the chocolate around gently, and then leave it to set.

When the shapes have been cut they can be decorated with a contrasting chocolate. Melt the chocolate in the usual way. Make some icing bags and snip the ends off. Use a no. 1 or 2 icing nozzle and carefully pipe patterns or edging on the cut-outs. Piping can be done without a nozzle, by just snipping the end from the icing bag when the chocolate is safely wrapped in, but your work will be neater and more controllable if one is used.

Coating Leaves

The leaves I prefer to use for coating are geranium, scented rose and lemon geranium, and peppermint. These all have prominent veins on their undersides, which make for good definition on the completed chocolate leaf. The scented geraniums also have interestingly shaped lobes. Rose leaves can be used but their veins are not quite so prominent.
1. Choose perfectly formed, unblemished leaves. If the plant has been growing outside, wash and dry the leaves very carefully. The leaves of pot plants do not require washing unless they have been sprayed with insecticide.
2. Lay the leaves, underside facing upwards, on a tray.
3. Melt the chocolate in the usual way.

*Photograph opposite, from top to bottom.
A selection of leaves coated with chocolate, including geranium, scented geranium and rose leaves.
Various shapes cut from blended chocolates have been decorated with piping.*

4. Hold the stem of a leaf and, using a skewer, spread the melted chocolate carefully over the surface, making sure all the crevices are covered.

5. Leave the chocolate to set in a cool room.

6. Rinse your wrists under the cold water tap for a few minutes. This will ensure your hands are cool, for the chocolate will soon melt if they are warm.

7. Hold the leaf stem and carefully peel it away from the chocolate. If, as with the more intricate geranium leaves, pieces of leaf tear and remain attached to the chocolate, use a needle or scalpel knife to ease them away.

8. The leaves are now ready to be used as decoration. An added bonus with scented geraniums is that the perfume mingles with the chocolate to give a delicate hint of lemon or rose.

The veins of leaves can be accentuated by piping them (using nozzle no. 1) in a contrasting colour. Allow the piping to set before you apply the main-colour chocolate.

Using Moulds

Apart from the Easter egg moulds, which can be bought at most good kitchenware shops, various plastic or metal food containers, or certain pre-moulded plastic packing, can be used. The little tubs which contain frozen desserts are also ideal.

All moulds must be scrupulously cleaned and dried, then polished with a piece of dry kitchen towel.

1. Melt the chocolate in the usual way. Remove it from the heat and leave it to cool for 5–10 minutes.

2. Pour the chocolate into the mould, twisting it around slowly in order to get an even coating.

3. Invert the mould on to a flat surface covered with aluminium foil or greaseproof paper.

4. Leave the chocolate to set in a cool room for 2–3 hours. As it sets it will come away slightly from the sides of the mould.

5. Melt some more chocolate and leave it to cool as before.

6. Pour the chocolate into the mould, making sure that all the 'set' chocolate is completely covered.

7. Invert the mould and leave to set as before.

8. If the mould is plastic, press it in slightly and push the chocolate out. If the mould is metal, tap it on the table or coax it out gently with the point of a knife.

The pre-moulded plastic trays, which are found in most boxes of chocolates, can be used to make your own chocolates. Here are some ideas:

1. Melt some plain, milk and white chocolate. Fill each little mould one-third full of plain chocolate and leave it to set. Add a one-third measure of milk chocolate, leave it to set, than add the white chocolate. When the chocolates are set, turn them out. The white layer will be at the bottom, so pipe simple swirls and lines in white, to contrast with the layer of plain chocolate at the top.

2. Coat the inside of each mould with chocolate, as described in the instructions for using moulds. Leave it to set, then half fill each cavity with any of the following: cherry jam, thick honey, a hazelnut, thick yoghurt or grated marzipan. Pour more chocolate over the filling and leave to set.

3. Fill the cavity (as described in previous paragraph) with an unusual home-made jelly – elderflower, scented geranium, rose

To make a traditional Easter egg, an egg-shaped mould is required. Two halves are made and when the egg has been filled with bonbons, the two sections are joined together with melted chocolate. The crazed surface on the mould enables the chocolate to be broken into manageable pieces!
Special moulds for hand-made chocolates come in various shapes and sizes.

petal, lime or peppermint. Use milk chocolate rather than plain as the latter will overpower the delicate flavour of the jellies.

4. Make exotic layered chocolates, as described in paragraph 1, by adding a few drops of essential oil to the milk chocolate – oil of jaffa, rose, lavender, sandalwood, ylang ylang, or frangipani. Freshly, finely ground cardamom seeds can also be added.

Leftovers, or Damaged Work

Work which has not quite come up to expectation, or which has been damaged, can be remelted and used later. Pieces of work which have developed the white bloom can also be remelted. Break the chocolate into pieces, melt in the usual way and pour into moulds – individual patty tins, the lower half of a butter dish or anything else that will hold the quantity. The moulds must be thoroughly washed and dried, then polished with a piece of kitchen paper. When the chocolate has set, carefully tap it out, wrap it in clingfilm then in aluminium foil, and store it in the refrigerator until required.

Storing Cut-Outs, Leaves and Moulds

These should be kept in an airtight container between layers of greaseproof paper. Large items could first be wrapped in clingfilm. Put the container somewhere cool and dry. The refrigerator is not really suitable because the sharp drop in temperature tends to cause the white bloom to develop on the surface of the chocolate.

Confectionery

Confectionery

Cherry brandy truffles

225g (8oz) plain chocolate
1 egg yoke
30g (1oz) butter
2 teasp cherry brandy
3 teasp single cream
110g (4oz) glacé cherries
approx. 30g (1oz) cocoa

1. Melt the chocolate in the usual way (page 15). Then remove from heat.
2. Stir in the egg yolk, butter, cherry brandy and cream.
3. Chop the cherries and mix thoroughly with other ingredients.
4. Refrigerate the mixture for 1 hour.
5. Sift the cocoa on to a plate. Drop a teaspoon of mixture into the cocoa and roll into a ball. Continue with the remaining mixture. Leave to set in a cool room.
6. Place the chocolates in fluted sweet cases. Store in an airtight container and refrigerate. Eat within 4–5 days.
Makes about 18.

Orange and honey truffles

110g (4oz) plain chocolate
110g (4oz) milk chocolate
3 tblsp thick honey
3 tblsp concentrated orange juice
3 tblsp double cream
Rind of 1 orange, finely grated
30g (1oz) cocoa
85g (3oz) granulated sugar
¼ teasp orange colouring

1. Melt the chocolate, together, in the usual way (page 15). Remove from heat.
2. Mix in the honey, orange juice and rind; then the cream.
3. Refrigerate the mixture for 1 hour.
4. Put the orange colouring into a basin. Add the sugar and mix until all the colour has been absorbed – the sugar should be slightly damp.
5. Sift the cocoa on to a plate. Drop 1 dessertspoonful of mixture into the cocoa, roll into a ball, then roll the ball in the coloured sugar and place in a fluted sweet case. The damp sugar will form a crisp coating. Continue with the remaining mixture.
6. Store in an airtight container and refrigerate. Eat within 4–5 days.
Makes about 25.

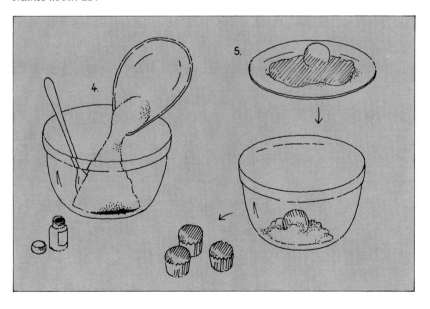

Almond truffles

170g (6oz) milk chocolate
280g (10oz) marzipan
2 teasp sherry
110g (4oz) chopped almonds

1. Melt the chocolate in the usual way (page 15). Remove from heat.
2. Break the marzipan into small pieces and mix it into the chocolate.
3. Stir in the sherry. Leave the mixture to stand for 5 minutes.
4. Using clean, dry hands, roll the mixture into balls, then roll each ball in the chopped almonds. Leave to set on a sheet of greaseproof paper, and then place in fluted sweet cases.
5. Store in an airtight container.
Makes about 24.

Chocolate fruit and nut honeys

55g (2oz) full fat soft cheese
2 tblsp thick honey
225g (8oz) icing sugar
55g (2oz) finely chopped nuts
6 chopped glacé cherries
6 chopped dried apricots
30g (1oz) cocoa
55g (2oz) plain chocolate

1. Beat the cheese and honey in a basin. Sift the icing sugar into the mixture.
2. Add the nuts, cherries and apricots. Mix thoroughly.
3. Sift the cocoa on to a plate. Take 1 dessertspoonful of mixture, drop it in the cocoa, roll into a ball and place in a fluted sweet case. Continue until all the mixture has been used.
4. Melt the chocolate in the usual way (page 15).
5. Spoon the chocolate into an icing bag fitted with a no. 3 icing nozzle. Pipe a round swirl on each chocolate.
6. Store in an airtight container and refrigerate. Eat within 3–4 days.
Makes about 26.

Photograph opposite and overleaf.
A selection of home-made chocolates makes a most welcome gift. The diagram on this page indicates each respective recipe.
1. Orange and honey truffles. 2. Almond truffles. 3. Nougat bonbons. 4. Chocolate ginger petits fours. 5. Chocolate mint creams. 6. Whisky coffee cups. 7. Cherry brandy truffles. 8. Chocolate marzipan cherries. 9. Dipped apricots. 10. Chocolate fruit and nut honeys.

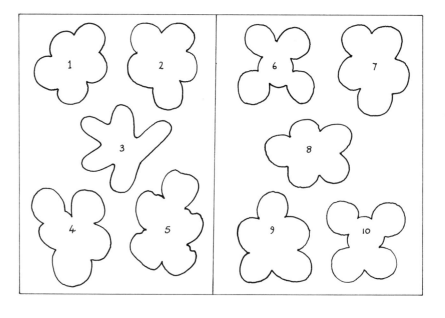

Chocolate marshmonds

10 marshmallows
55g (2oz) chopped almonds
225g (8oz) plain chocolate

1. Line a 130mm (5in.) square baking tin with waxed paper.
2. Chop the marshmallows into small pieces (or use scissors dusted with icing sugar).
3. Melt the chocolate in the usual way (page 15). Remove from heat and leave to cool for 10 minutes.
4. Stir in the almonds and marshmallows, then pour the mixture into the tin. Use the back of a spoon to smooth the surface and push the mixture into the corners.
5. When the chocolate is almost set, lift it out of the tin.
6. Using a long, sharp knife, cut the block into 16 squares, then cut each square across diagonally.
7. Store in an airtight container, in a cool dry place.
Makes 32.

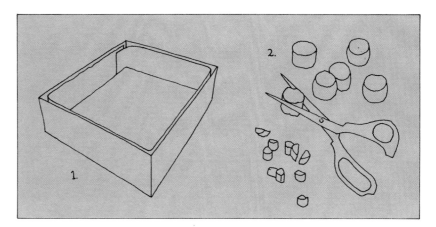

Whisky coffee cups

225g (8oz) milk chocolate
2½ teasp quality instant coffee
1 tblsp water
30g (1oz) soft butter, chopped
1 egg yolk
2 teasp whisky
55g (2oz) shelled hazelnuts

1. Melt 140g (5oz) of the chocolate in the usual way (page 15).
2. Arrange about 26 fluted sweet cases on a baking sheet.
3. Drop 1 teaspoonful of the melted chocolate into a sweet case. Place another inside the first and press gently so that the chocolate comes up the sides.
4. Continue until all the melted chocolate has been used. Refrigerate for 1 hour.
5. Melt the remaining chocolate as before. Remove from heat.
6. Dissolve the coffee in the water and stir it into the chocolate.
7. When the mixture has cooled a little, beat in the butter, egg yolk and whisky.
8. Carefully remove both paper cups from each chocolate.
9. Drop some of the mixture into each chocolate cup and top with a hazelnut.
10. Store in an airtight container and refrigerate. Eat within 4–5 days.
Makes about 26.

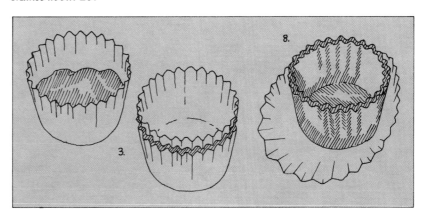

Chocolate ginger petits fours

30g (1oz) plain chocolate
1 small egg white
55g (2oz) caster sugar
85g (3oz) finely chopped nuts
½ teasp ginger powder
280g (10oz) milk chocolate

1. Refrigerate the plain chocolate.
2. Preheat the oven to cool (the lowest temperature).
3. Lightly oil 2 baking sheets.
4. Remove the plain chocolate from the refrigerator and grate finely.
5. Beat the egg white until it is stiff. Fold in 30g (1oz) of the sugar, the nuts, ginger and grated chocolate.
6. Sprinkle the working surface with the remaining sugar and flatten the mixture to 6mm (¼in.) thick. Using petits fours cutters, cut out the shapes. Re-roll the trimmings and continue until all the mixture has been used.
7. Place the shapes on the baking trays and bake for 30 minutes.
8. Remove and leave to cool on a wire rack.
9. Melt the milk chocolate in the usual way (page 15).
10. Position a sheet of greaseproof paper under a wire tray. Dip each of the shapes (see page 16 for dipping) and place them carefully on the wire tray.
11. When all the shapes have been covered, start again at the beginning and, using a corn-cob fork, mark each one four times, lifting a string of chocolate up each time and carrying it forward to the next mark.
12. Leave to set. Store in an airtight container in a cool dry place.
Makes about 50.

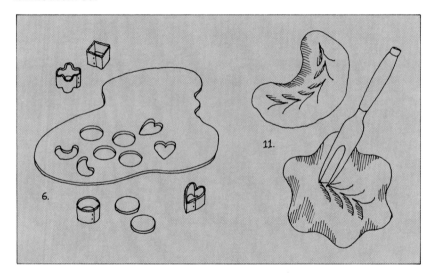

Chocolate marzipan cherries

110g (4oz) glacé cherries
225g (8oz) marzipan
170g (6oz) plain chocolate
7g (¼oz) vegetable shortening

1. Cut the cherries in half.
2. Roll the marzipan into 24 even-sized balls, then flatten each one.
3. Put half a cherry on each piece of marzipan and wrap it neatly around to form a smooth ball.
4. Melt the chocolate in the usual way (page 15), and stir in the shortening.
5. Dip each marzipan ball into the chocolate (see page 16 for dipping).
6. When the chocolates have set, place in fluted sweet cases. Store in an airtight container between layers of waxed paper.
Makes 24.

Nougat bonbons

1 egg white
2 tblsp thick honey
pinch of cream of tartar
110ml (4fl. oz) water
170g (6oz) granulated sugar
1½ tblsp liquid glucose
45g (1½oz) chopped glacé cherries
30g (1oz) chopped almonds
4 tblsp icing sugar
225g (8oz) plain chocolate
85g (3oz) milk chocolate

1. Beat the egg white until it is stiff; then beat in the honey and cream of tartar.
2. Put the sugar and water in a heavy-based pan and simmer until the sugar dissolves.
3. Add the glucose, then boil to 132°C. (270°F.).
4. Remove from heat. Stirring continuously, add the egg white mixture. Beat the mixture for 20 minutes, then stir in the cherries and nuts.
5. Dust the working surface with icing sugar, turn out the nougat and, with dusted hands, form them into small rolls. Leave on a dusted surface for 2–3 hours (the rolls will spread a little).
6. Melt the plain chocolate in the usual way. Re-roll each bonbon and cover with the melted chocolate (see page 16 for dipping).
7. Melt the milk chocolate (page 15). Make an icing bag, and with nozzle no. 2 pipe continuous horizontal lines on each bonbon. Start at the beginning again and pipe a central vertical line on each bonbon.
8. When each bonbon is set, place them in a fluted sweet case and store between layers of waxed paper in an airtight container.
Makes 30 to 40.

Chocolate nutty fudge

425ml (¾pt) sweetened condensed milk
450g (1lb) granulated sugar
2 tblsp clear honey
110g (4oz) chopped butter
1 teasp vanilla essence
110g (4oz) chopped hazelnuts
110g (4oz) plain chocolate, grated

1. Lightly grease a 180mm × 280mm (7in. × 11in.) shallow baking tin.
2. Place the condensed milk, sugar, honey and butter in a heavy-based pan. Bring to the boil and, stirring continuously, allow the mixture to boil for 10 minutes.
3. Remove from heat and add the essence, nuts and chocolate. Beat vigorously until the mixture thickens, then quickly pour it into the greased tin.
4. When the fudge is almost cold mark it into squares. When it is completely cold, cut the squares and remove from the tin.
5. Store the fudge in an airtight jar or tin between layers of waxed paper.
Makes about 40.

Banana chocolate fudge

335g (12oz) granulated sugar
170g (6oz) soft brown sugar
140ml (¼pt) milk
140g (5oz) milk chocolate
1 tblsp clear honey
1 large firm banana, mashed
140g (5oz) chopped butter
55g (2oz) walnuts, finely chopped

1. Grease a 200mm × 250mm (8in. × 10in.) baking tin.
2. Put the sugars, milk, honey, chocolate and butter into a heavy-based pan. Heat gently, stirring continuously.
3. Add the banana and bring the mixture to boil, stirring occasionally, until the temperature reaches 116°C. (240°F.).
4. Remove from heat, then beat until the fudge thickens or begins to turn grainy. Pour immediately into the baking tin and, while still warm, press the chopped walnuts into the surface. Mark into squares. When the fudge is cold and set firm, cut into pieces and store in an airtight container between layers of waxed paper.
Makes about 40.

Chocolate mint creams

approx. 225g (8oz) icing sugar
1 egg white
4 drops peppermint essence
green colouring
red colouring
85g (3oz) plain chocolate

1. Put the egg white into a basin and beat for a few minutes. Gradually fold in the icing sugar.
2. Dust the working surface with icing sugar, turn the paste out, and knead.
3. Divide the paste into three portions. Add a few drops of green to one portion and knead thoroughly. Add a few drops of red to the second portion and knead.
4. Cover the two portions with a clean tea towel. Then, using a dusted rolling pin, roll the third portion to 3mm (⅛in.) thick. Cut little hearts with a cocktail cutter. Re-roll the trimmings and continue cutting until all the paste has been used. Leave to set on a dusted surface.
5. Repeat with the two remaining portions.
6. Melt the chocolate in the usual way (page 15). Using an icing bag fitted with nozzle no. 1, pipe decoration as shown in the diagram.
7. When the piping has set, store the mints in an airtight container between layers of waxed paper.
Makes about 25.

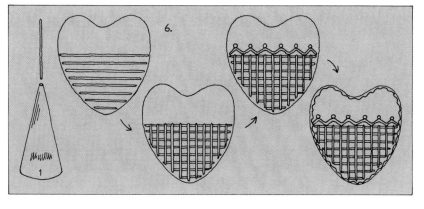

Photograph opposite.
The diagram on this page indicates each respective recipe.
1. Banana chocolate fudge. 2. Chocolate marshmonds. 3. Chocolate nutty fudge. 4. Chewy chocolate caramels.

Dipped apricots

225g (8oz) moisturised dried apricots
85g (3oz) whole unblanched almonds
225g (8oz) milk chocolate
85g (3oz) plain chocolate

1. Melt the milk chocolate in the usual way (page 15).
2. Slide an almond into the cavity of each apricot, then press the edges together.
3. Coat each apricot with the melted chocolate and place them carefully on waxed paper (see page 16 for dipping).
4. When the chocolate has set, melt the plain chocolate and, using nozzle no. 2, pipe the flower pattern as shown.
5. Leave to set, then store in an airtight container between layers of waxed paper.
Makes about 30.

Chewy chocolate caramels

285ml (½pt) single cream
110g (4oz) cocoa
200g (7oz) golden syrup
225g (8oz) granulated sugar

1. Pour the cream into a large heavy-based pan. Add the cocoa and sugar, then dissolve on a low heat. Stir continuously and add the golden syrup.
2. Bring the mixture slowly to boil and cook gently for about 45 minutes, stirring occasionally to prevent sticking.
3. Thoroughly grease a 200mm × 250mm (8in. × 10in.) baking tin.
4. When the mixture has reduced and become thick, pour it into the tin.
5. After 10 minutes mark the toffee into 40 squares.
6. When the toffee is completely cold, slip a knife around the edge of the tin and peel the whole slab out. Using oiled scissors, cut the 40 pieces, then roll them into smooth balls.
7. Place the balls in fluted sweet cases and store in an airtight container.
Makes 40.

Chocolate Creations

Chocolate Creations

Easter egg

approx. 450g (1lb) plain chocolate
170g (6oz) marzipan
1 teasp cocoa
170g (6oz) icing sugar
¼ egg white
¼ teasp gum tragacanth
Green, blue, yellow and orange food colouring

Large plastic Easter egg mould
Aluminium foil
Greaseproof paper
Silicone paper
Basket net nail
Bekenal (or equivalent) icing nozzles, 2, 3, 4 and 37
Ateco (or equivalent) nozzle 78

Note. Approximate weights are given for chocolate but, it is better to have too much than too little. Beginners will find the Easter egg easier to unmould when two or three layers of chocolate have been applied. During the periods waiting for the egg to set, follow instructions 9 to 22, making the marzipan ring, the royal icing flower basket and the chocolate decorations.

1. To make the first half of the egg: melt the chocolate in the usual way (page 15). Meanwhile, wash and dry the mould, and polish it thoroughly with kitchen paper towel.
2. Spoon the melted chocolate into the mould. Twist it around to give an even coating. Continue to add more chocolate and twist until the mould is completely covered.

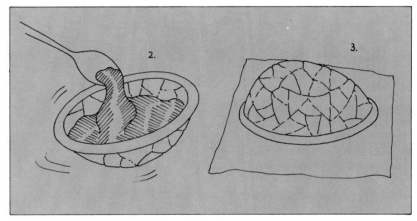

3. Invert the mould on to a flat surface covered with aluminium foil. Set in a cool room, or refrigerate, until set.
4. Re-melt the chocolate, remove from heat, and leave to cool for 5 minutes.
5. Pour or spoon the chocolate into the mould, twisting as before, then smooth the surface with the back of the spoon. Make sure that all the 'set' chocolate is completely covered.
6. Invert the mould on to the foil and leave it to set again. As the chocolate sets it will come away slightly from the sides of the mould.
7. Ease the chocolate out of the mould by gently pushing it in the centre until a slight cracking noise can be heard. The chocolate should then drop out. (My first attempt at this was disastrous. The chocolate refused to move – because I had not polished the mould sufficiently. So I held the mould under hot water, as one would for jelly, which naturally melted all the chocolate!)
8. Keep this half egg in a cool place covered with a dry cloth. Repeat instructions 1 to 7 for the other half.
9. Knead the marzipan until soft and pliable. Flatten it out and sprinkle with cocoa. Knead again until the cocoa is thoroughly blended.
10. Pull the marzipan out evenly to a length of 370mm (14½in.) and join to form an oval shape. Leave to dry on a sheet of greaseproof paper dusted with icing sugar.

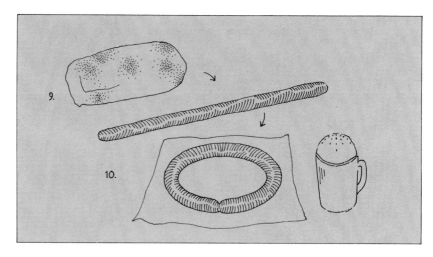

11. To make the tragacanth icing, pour the egg white on to a saucer; then take as near to three-quarters of it as possible, and pour it into a clean basin.

12. Sieve the icing sugar and tragacanth over the egg white, and beat it until smooth. This can be done by hand, or in the mixer using a beater rather than a whisk, on the slowest speed. The correct consistency can really only be judged after a little practice with the icing bag – it should not be too runny to lose its shape, or too stiff to flow easily from the bag.

13. Take the basket nail and coat the surface evenly with lard.

14. Make an icing bag (page 17) and insert nozzle no. 3. Pipe vertical lines down the sides of the basket, then 5 horizontal lines all the way round, pushing gently into one side of each vertical line.

15. Using nozzle no. 2 pipe vertical lines, between the previous vertical lines, to give an overall basket effect.

16. Using no. 3 again fill the base of the basket in with a continuous zigzag line. Finish with 2 rows of continuous dots around the top and bottom edges. Stick the nail into a potato (or orange etc) and leave until set.

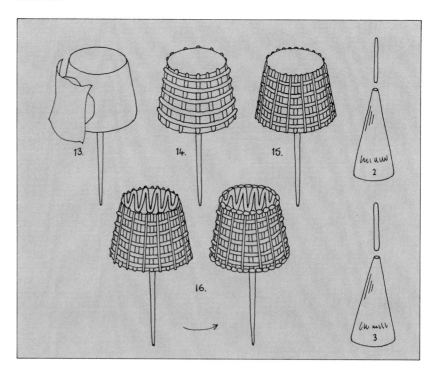

A basket made from piped icing supports two halves of an Easter egg, positioned to reveal a riot of icing flowers.
This would be a very special Easter gift for someone near and dear.

17. Colour some of the icing different shades of green (by adding blue or yellow to the green) and pipe supports for the flowers. Pipe directly on to waxed or silicone paper, or foil, as shown. When these have dried they will be positioned in the basket, secured with blobs of icing, and the flower heads will be piped straight on to them.

18. Trace the chocolate decoration design on to a sheet of white paper and cover with silicone paper. Tape both papers on to a tray or ridged surface. Melt some chocolate and, using nozzle no. 2, pipe the shapes. You will need 17 full designs, 68 pieces in all. Leave the designs to dry.

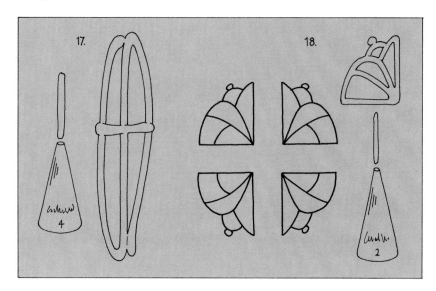

19. When the basket has dried, carefully fill the mould, to the brim, with very hot water. The lard will melt and after one or two little cracking noises, the basket will come away from the mould.

20. Position the flower supports in the basket, securing them with blobs of icing. Using the 2 flower nozzles and yellow and orange icing, pipe flower heads on to the supports. Leave to dry.

21. Position the egg halves in the marzipan ring and pour some melted chocolate into the base. When this has set, carefully place the basket in position. Attach the chocolate decorations to the egg and marzipan ring (as shown in the photograph) with discreet blobs of melted chocolate. Then pipe a large blob in the centre of each of the egg decorations.

Bird cage

225g (8oz) icing sugar
1 egg white
½ teasp gum tragacanth

110g (4oz) sunflower margarine
85g (3oz) soft brown sugar
2 eggs
110g (4oz) self-raising flour
30g (1oz) cocoa powder

------

3 × 225g (8oz) boxes fondant
or to make your own
670g (1½lb) icing sugar
1½ egg whites
3 tblsp liquid glucose

------

mild honey

55g (2oz) marzipan
½ teasp cocoa

------

approx. 110g (4oz) plain chocolate
approx. 55g (2oz) milk chocolate

------

1 × 130mm (5in.) square cake tin
Greaseproof paper
Ateco (or equivalent) nozzles no. 1, 2, 4, 82
Plain white sheets A4 paper
Silicone paper
Adhesive tape
Tall drinking glass

1. To make the tragacanth icing, pour the egg white into a clean basin. Sieve the icing sugar and tragacanth over the egg white and beat until smooth – this can be done by hand, or in the mixer using a beater rather than a whisk, on the slowest speed. The correct consistency can only be judged after a little practice with the icing bag – it should not be too runny to lose its shape, or too stiff to flow easily from the bag. Add 2–3 drops of colouring and beat until thoroughly blended. Cover the basin with a damp cloth.
2. Trace the side and roof sections on to 4 sheets of paper. One of the side-sections should have an opening for the door, as shown. The door can be traced on to one of the four sheets.

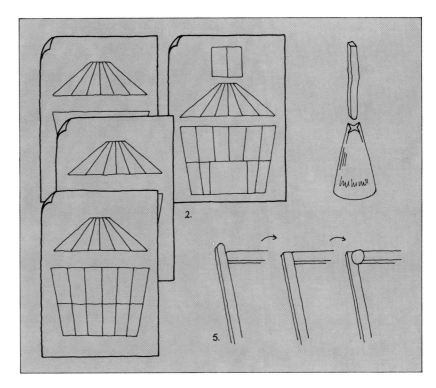

3. Tape the sheets on to a table, then tape a sheet of silicone paper over the top.
4. Make an icing bag (page 17), insert nozzle no. 82, and spoon in some of the icing.
5. Carefully pipe the cage sections, making sure that all vertical lines are attached securely to the horizontal ones. Neaten the joins with the point of a sharp knife. Finish with a dot to cover each join. Leave the sections to dry, preferably overnight. (It is always a good idea to make one or two spare sections in case of accident.)
6. To make the chocolate cake, lightly grease and line the tin with greaseproof paper. Preheat the oven to 190°C. (375°F., gas mark 5).
7. Sieve the flour and cocoa into a basin.
8. Beat the sugar and margarine in another basin until it is pale brown, smooth and creamy.
9. Beat the eggs into the margarine, one at a time, following each with a tablespoonful of the flour/cocoa mixture. Fold in the remaining flour.
10. Spoon the mixture into the prepared tin. Smooth the surface and set it on the centre shelf of the oven for 30–35 minutes, or until firm on top and coming away slightly from the sides of the tin.
11. Leave the cake in the tin for 5–10 minutes, then transfer the cake to a wire tray, first removing the lining paper, and leave until cold.

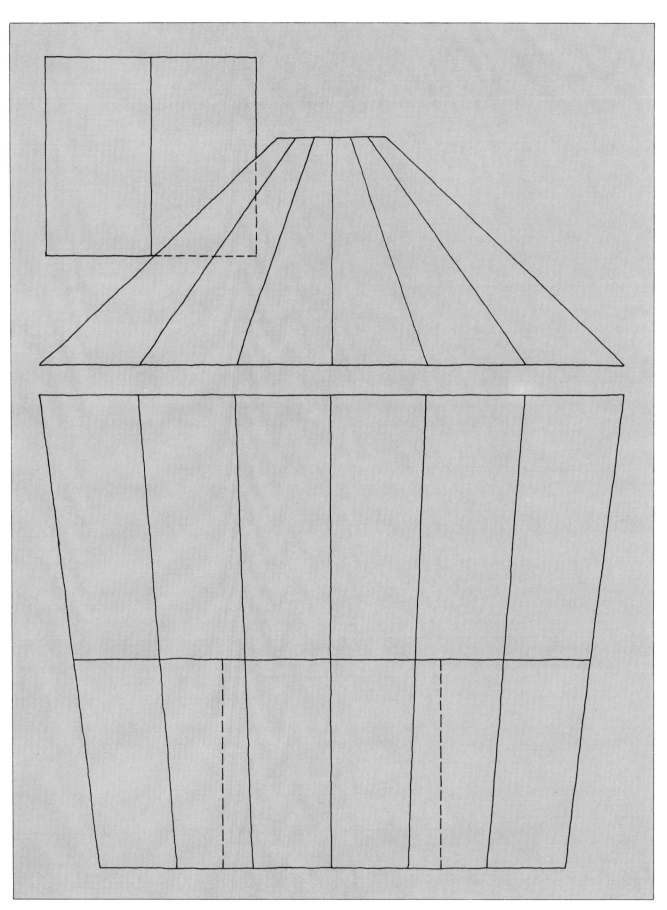

12. Ready-made commercial fondant can be bought in 226g (8oz) blocks from cake-decorating specialists and some supermarkets. To make your own, drop the 1½ egg whites into a basin and slowly mix in the sieved icing sugar and warmed liquid glucose. The quantities of icing sugar and egg white are not absolutely critical, more or less of one or the other may be needed to achieve the correct consistency which should be easy and firm to work with. If it feels floppy, add some more sieved icing sugar; if it becomes difficult to handle, add a little more egg white.

13. Dust a working surface with icing sugar. Use the fondant in 2 halves for easier handling. Roll to 8mm (⁵⁄₁₆in.) thick, then cut pieces to fit the 4 sides and the top.

14. Brush the cake with mild clear honey and carefully attach the sides, then the top. Leave the cake on one side.

15. Flatten the marzipan and sprinkle it with the cocoa. Knead until the cocoa is thoroughly blended, then model into a bird shape, as shown. Leave the bird to dry on a dusted surface.

16. Trace the filigree design on to paper 4 times. Tape to the table and cover with silicone paper as before.

17. Melt the plain chocolate in the usual way (page 15). Remove from heat and leave to cool for 5 minutes. Make an icing bag, insert nozzle no. 2 and spoon in some of the melted chocolate.

18. Follow the lines of the design carefully. Do not overlap the lines. Where one crosses another, stop, then start again at the other side.

19. Using the same nozzle, pipe small designs on to the cage pieces, as shown. Pipe wings and tail feathers on the marzipan bird. (The eyes on the bird were piped with blue icing from the chocolate box illustrated on page 51. Chocolate eyes will do just as well.)

20. When the filigree designs have set, put a generous teaspoonful of icing in a saucer. Add a drop of water and mix to a creamy but runny consistency. Using a very small spoon or skewer, fill in the areas of the design as shown on the photograph.

21. Using nozzle no. 1 pipe a line of continuous dots between the 2 lines of chocolate which frame the design.

22. Melt the milk chocolate. Remove from heat and leave to cool for 5 minutes. Make an icing bag, insert nozzle no. 4 and pipe a continuous line of dots over the fondant seam around the top edge of the cake.

23. When the icing on the filigree designs has set, attach them carefully to each side of the cake. Secure, using discreet blobs of icing behind the filled-in areas. (This can be done before or after erecting the cage.)

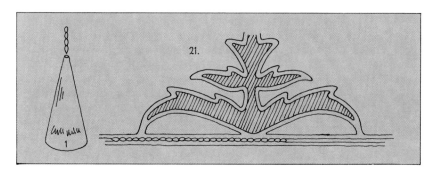

24. You will need some tall items to support the cage sides while assembling, e.g. cereal boxes. Using nozzle no. 4, pipe a line of icing along 2 adjoining sides of the cake top. Stick 2 sides into the icing, leaning slightly out, then support them.

25. Pipe a line of icing inside the join, and up the join of the 2 sides, as shown.

26. Repeat with the remaining sides, after leaving the first and second for a while to dry.

27. Using the same nozzle, pipe a line of continuous dots, for added strength, around the bottom and up the sides of the cage.

28. Position the bird just inside the cage. Pipe a line of icing just inside the door opening. Attach the door, supporting it with a jar or cup, until secure.

29. Position a glass tumbler on the centre of the cake and fill it with sweets or chocolate buttons, flowers, or any decoration appropriate to the occasion.

30. Position the roof pieces, and support them by the cage sides and the top of the tumbler. These can be secured with icing or left loose.

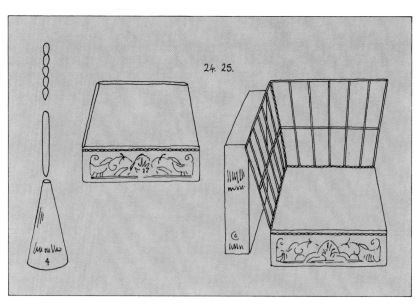

Photograph opposite.
Not a bird in a gilded cage but one made entirely from fondant icing and chocolate! The chocolate cake base is topped with fondant icing and the bird is modelled from chocolate flavoured marzipan.

Chocolate box

280g–335g (10oz–12oz) plain chocolate
approx. 110g (4oz) milk chocolate
110g (4oz) icing sugar
½ egg white
¼ teasp gum tragacanth
Blue food colouring

Heart-shaped cocktail cutter
Heart-shaped biscuit cutter
Bekenal (or equivalent) icing nozzles no. 2, 4
Sheets of plain white A4 paper
Silicone paper
Adhesive tape

1. Make the tragacanth icing. Pour an egg white into a saucer and take as near as possible to half of it and slide it into a clean basin.
2. Sieve the icing sugar and tragacanth over the egg white, then beat until smooth. This can be done by hand, or in the mixer using a beater rather than a whisk, on the slowest speed. The correct consistency can only be judged after a little practice with the icing bag – it should not be too runny to lose its shape, or too stiff to flow easily from the bag.
3. Colour the icing with 2–3 drops of colouring. Mix thoroughly, then cover with a damp cloth until required.
4. Trace the box shapes on to the white paper. You will be able to fit 8 side pieces (pipe 2 extra) on to 2 sheets, the 6 lid pieces on to another and the hexagonal base on to another.

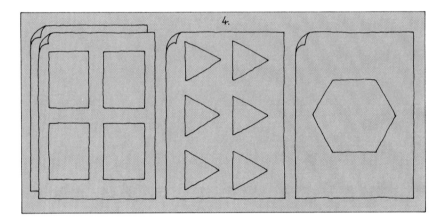

5. Tape the paper on to a table or working surface. Tape a piece of silicone paper over the top.
6. Make an icing bag (page 17) and insert nozzle no. 4. Following the lines of each shape, pipe each one, neatening the final join of each by careful trimming with the sharp point of a knife. Leave the frames to dry, about 3–4 hours.

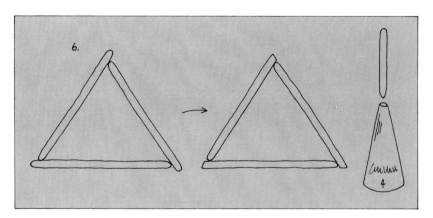

7. Melt the chocolate in the usual way (page 15). Remove from heat and leave to cool for 5 minutes. Carefully pour the chocolate into each frame, smoothing the surface with the back of a spoon. Leave to set.
8. Peel each piece carefully from the silicone paper and turn it over, to work on the flat side. Using the biscuit cutter, cut a heart from the side pieces. Using the cocktail cutter, cut a heart from each of the lid pieces. (This is easier if you warm the cutters, just a little, before cutting into the chocolate. Stand them in a bowl of hot water, remove and dry. This should be repeated for each cut).

12.

9. Using nozzle no. 4 for the side pieces, pipe a row of continuous dots around the edge of the heart shape. Repeat for the lid pieces, using nozzle no. 2.

10. Using the same nozzle, pipe a row of continuous dots around each piece, between the frame and the chocolate. Leave to set.

11. Trace the filigree design on to a sheet of A4 paper, 6 times. Tape it to the table or a tray, cover it with silicone paper as before, and secure it with tape.

12. Melt the milk chocolate in the usual way (page 15). Make an icing bag, insert nozzle no. 2 and pipe the decorations. Leave to set.

13. The chocolate decorations can be attached to the side-pieces before or after assembly. Use discreet blobs of chocolate to secure.

14. Assembling the box takes a little time and patience. You will need some small jars or boxes, anything small with some weight to it, to support each piece as it is erected. Also have an icing bag ready fitted with no. 4 nozzle and plenty of icing.

15. Pipe a line of icing on one side of the base, as shown. Prop one of the side-pieces against it, then pipe another line to secure the piece. Support it with a weight. Repeat with the next side-piece, then pipe a line to secure the two pieces together.

16. Repeat this with all the pieces until they are all in place, taking time between each one to allow the icing to set a little.

17. Pipe rows of continuous dots around the base and down the join of each side-piece.

18. When the icing is completely set, fill the box carefully with wrapped sweets or chocolates. These will act as supports for the lid until the icing attaching them to the box has set.

19. Pipe a line of icing on one side of the top of the box. Position a lid piece into the icing. Continue until all pieces are in position.

20. Pipe a line of continuous dots along each join, then pipe a large dot between and at the tip of each lid. Leave to set.

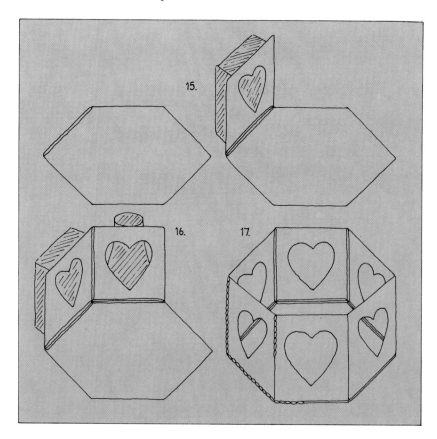

This box made of chocolate has cut-out heart shapes on the side and top sections to reveal a selection of chocolates. Wrap each chocolate in glittering silver paper before placing it in the box.

Christmas crackers

approx. 225g (8oz) plain chocolate
approx. 55g (2oz) milk chocolate
55g (2oz) icing sugar
¼ of an egg white
15g (½oz) marzipan
Red and green food colouring

------

2 tubes from kitchen paper towel
Scalpel knife
Aluminium foil
Adhesive tape
Double-sided adhesive tape
Ateco (or equivalent) icing nozzles, 1, 2 and 3
2 sheets white A4 paper
Silicone paper
Rolling pin

1. Draw a straight line on both sides of the towel tube, dividing it exactly in half. Draw 2 lines around the tube, dividing it in to three but making the centre portion 20mm (¾in.) larger than the outer ones –approximately 70mm, 90mm, 70mm (2⅘in., 3⅗in., 2⅘in.).

2. Using the scalpel knife, cut the tube carefully into thirds, using the pencil lines as guides.

3. Pencil a line 10mm (⅜in.) in from the edge of one of the shorter tubes. Score this line (being careful not to penetrate the card completely) so that it will bend easily. Now make cuts approximately 10mm (⅜in.) apart, up to the scored line, as shown.

4. Bend the cut pieces inwards, each piece overlapping the next. Secure with thin strips of adhesive tape.

5. Repeat instructions 3 and 4 for the other short tube, then with both sides of the middle tube.

6. Using the pencil lines as guides cut the middle tube carefully in half.

7. Cut a length of foil 20mm (¾in.) wider than the length of each short tube. Fold it into narrow pleats. Stretch it out, as shown, then cut in half. Fold each half round to form a tube, and secure it with adhesive tape.

8. Attach a length of adhesive tape (double-sided) to the uncut inside edge of each of the short tubes, then push the pleated foil tube in. Press the pleats gently against the adhesive tape. Turn the excess foil neatly over.

9. Line the 2 halves of the large tube with foil.

10. Repeat instructions 1 to 10 for the other towel tube.

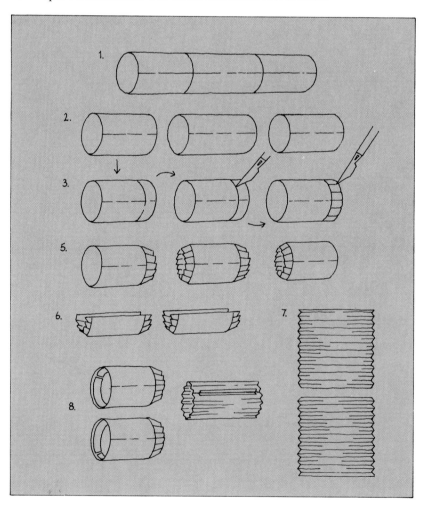

11. Melt the plain chocolate in the usual way (page 15). Remove from heat and spoon it carefully into the foil lined tubes, twisting slowly to ensure that the pleats are well coated. Use the spoon handle or a skewer to help. Stand the tubes upright, on foil, to set.

12. Coat the halved tubes with the chocolate, then invert them on to foil and leave them to set.

13. Meanwhile, make the royal icing. Break the egg white on to a saucer then take as near to a quarter of it as possible, and pour it into a clean bowl.

14. Sieve the icing sugar over the egg white and beat until smooth. Cover with a damp cloth until required.

15. Trace the holly on to a sheet of white paper 4 times. Cover with a sheet of silicone paper. Colour half the icing green. Make an icing bag (page 17), insert nozzle no. 2, and 2 teaspoonsful of icing, then pipe the outline of the holly. Leave to dry for about 30 minutes.

16. Mix 2 or 3 drops of water with the remaining green icing and, using a skewer or very small spoon, carefully fill in the holly.

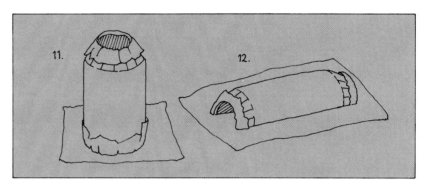

These chocolate crackers capture all the magic of Christmas and would grace any table. Keep them refrigerated until just before the meal is to be served, then make sure that they are not placed too near hot plates or dishes.

17. Remove the silicone paper and cut it into squares, each square supporting a holly leaf. Attach 2 squares, crosswise, to the rolling pin with adhesive tape, as shown. Attach the other 2 to the inside of a cup, lying on its side. Leave to set.

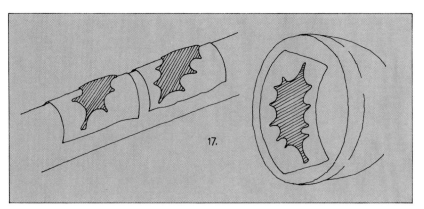

18. Trace the pattern on to a sheet of paper 4 times. Attach the paper to the table with adhesive tape. Cover with silicone paper and secure with tape.
19. Re-melt the chocolate, then remove it from heat and leave to cool for 5 minutes. Make an icing bag and insert nozzle no. 2. Spoon in the melted chocolate and pipe the decorations. When these have set leave them as they are or paint with edible gold food colouring – available in powdered form from some cake-decorating specialists.
20. Knead the red colouring into the marzipan and make 6 or 7 little berries. Leave on a dusted surface to dry.
21. Using the scalpel, carefully cut away the tubes and foil. Re-melt the plain chocolate and assemble the crackers, using the melted chocolate to secure. A little gift can be placed in the hollow centre-piece.
22. Using nozzle no. 1 and the melted chocolate, pipe a circle of continuous dots on top of each cracker – use a round cocktail cutter to imprint the circle.

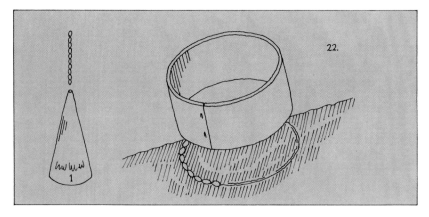

23. Position the 5 designs over the joins of the crackers, as shown on the photograph, securing with melted chocolate.
24. Melt the milk chocolate in the usual way. Using nozzle no. 3, pipe a row of continuous dots along the seams and over the tops of the centre-pieces, as shown in the photograph.
25. Fill the chocolate circle, on top of the crackers, with runny white icing (as with the holly). When the icing has almost set, attach the holly leaves and berries.

Geranium tree

approx. 660g (20oz) plain chocolate
approx. 110g (4oz) each of milk chocolate and
white chocolate
55g (2oz) icing sugar
¼ of an egg white
Orange and green food colouring

Large plastic Easter egg mould
Scalpel knife
Pliable card
Adhesive tape
Aluminium foil
Greaseproof paper
Bekenal (or equivalent) icing nozzles 37 and 4
Scented geranium leaves

1. Cut the card to 380mm (15in.) long and 100mm (4in.) deep. Roll into a tube 50mm (2in.) diameter. Secure with a strip of adhesive tape down the side. Make cuts at both ends, as shown. Splay the cuts out and secure with tape.
2. Cut a piece of foil about 40mm (1½in.) longer than the tube. Crinkle the foil to resemble bark, then line the tube, folding excess foil neatly over the edges.
3. Cut a circle of card to fit one end of the tube. Cover with foil and attach securely with tape.
4. Melt the plain chocolate in the usual way (page 15). Meanwhile wash and dry the Easter egg mould, then polish it thoroughly with kitchen paper towel.
5. Spoon the melted chocolate into the mould. Twist it round to give an even coating. Continue to add more chocolate, twisting until the mould is completely covered.
6. Invert the mould on to a flat surface covered with aluminium foil. Keep in a cool room or refrigerate until set.
7. Carefully spoon some of the chocolate into the tube, twisting as before, to ensure complete coverage. Turn the tube upright and leave to set.

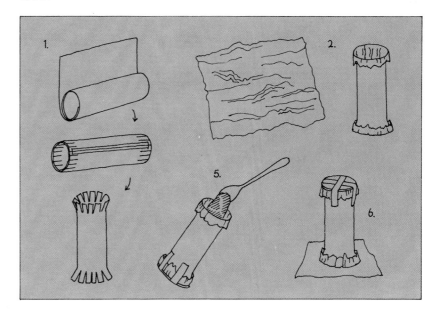

8. Re-melt the chocolate, remove from heat and leave to cool for 5 minutes.
9. Pour the chocolate into the egg mould, twisting as before, then smooth the surface with the back of a spoon. Make sure all the 'set' chocolate is completely covered. Invert the mould and leave to set.
10. Give the tube a second lining of chocolate, again making sure the previous coating is completely covered. Leave to set.
11. Ease the egg out of the mould by gently pushing it in the centre until a slight cracking sound can be heard. Keep the half-egg in a cool place covered with a dry cloth. Wash, dry and polish the mould, then repeat instructions 5 and 6 for the other half.
12. Join the 2 egg halves together with melted chocolate. (A small bag of sweets or any other little surprise can be placed inside before the joining, but nothing too heavy.)
13. Using the scalpel knife, remove the base of the tube, then slit the tube and carefully peel away the foil.
14. Stand the trunk upright (handle the chocolate carefully, using a dry cloth) and attach the egg, using melted chocolate to secure.

15. Cut the unblemished leaves from the scented geranium plant, a couple at a time, leaving some stem to hold. If the plant has been growing out of doors or been sprayed with insecticide, the leaves should be washed and dried. Washing should be avoided as it tends to make the leaves limp. It is not necessary if the plant has been growing indoors.

16. Melt the white and milk chocolate and re-melt the plain. Mix the chocolates in 4 bowls to make 4 shades of brown – dark, medium dark, medium and pale.

17. Lay the leaves, underside facing upwards, on the table. Hold the stem of a leaf and, using a skewer, spread the melted chocolate carefully over the leaf, going to the edges and making sure all the tiny crevices are filled. Leave to set in a cool room or refrigerate.

18. Rinse your hands under the cold water tap for a few minutes – this will ensure cold hands. The chocolate will easily mark or melt if you have warm ones.

19. Holding the leaf stem, carefully peel it away from the chocolate. If pieces of leaf tear and remain attached to the chocolate, use the scalpel knife or a needle to ease them off.

20. Start at the top of the egg and secure each leaf with melted chocolate. The leaf will need to be held on (with cold fingers) for a few seconds until the chocolate sets.

21. Break the egg white into a saucer. Take as near a quarter of it as possible, and pour it into a basin. Sieve the icing sugar over the egg white and mix thoroughly until smooth.

22. Divide the icing in half, colour one half with orange colouring, the other half with green.

23. Make 2 icing bags (see page 17) and insert the 2 nozzles. Pipe little buds and flowers at various places in the chocolate foliage. Leave to set.

24. Secure the tree, using melted chocolate, to a round silver cake board. Place 3 or 4 chocolate leaves around the tree.

Photograph opposite.
This tree has a chocolate trunk and is topped with an Easter egg, which is covered with chocolate coated geranium leaves to represent the foliage.
The foliage is then dotted with buds and flowers, using piped icing sugar.

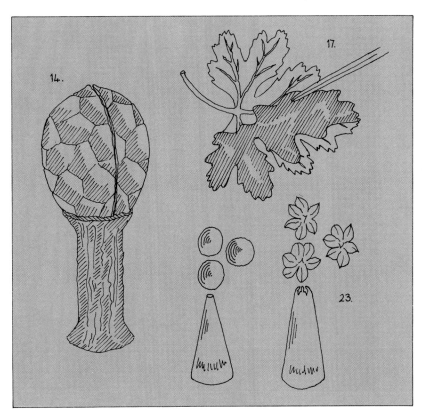

Cabbage flower

110g (4oz) sunflower margarine
85g (3oz) soft brown sugar
2 eggs
110g (4oz) self-raising flour
30g (1oz) cocoa

335g (12oz) marzipan
30g (1oz) cocoa
mild clear honey

------

1 small hard cabbage
approx. 85g (3oz) plain chocolate
approx. 170g (6oz) milk chocolate
approx. 225g (8oz) white chocolate
Red food colouring

Greaseproof paper
200mm (8in.) round sandwich cake tin
Ateco (or equivalent) icing nozzle no. 4

Photograph opposite.
The chocolate cake base of this confection is covered with marzipan. Cabbage leaves are coated with pale, medium and dark chocolate to represent the petals of a flower and the stamens are piped with white chocolate.

1. To make the chocolate cake, lightly grease and line the tin with greaseproof paper. Preheat the oven to 190°C (375°F., gas mark 5).
2. Sieve the flour and cocoa into a basin.
3. Beat the sugar and margarine in another basin until pale brown, smooth and creamy.
4. Beat the eggs into the margarine, one at a time, following each with a tablespoonful of the flour/cocoa mixture. Fold in the remaining flour.
5. Spoon the mixture into the prepared tin. Smooth the surface and place on the centre shelf of the oven for 30–35 minutes, or until firm on top and coming away slightly from the sides of the tin.
6. Leave the cake in the tin for 5–10 minutes, then transfer the cake to a wire tray, first removing the lining paper, and leave until cold.
7. Slice any bumps from the top of the cake, then turn it over.
8. Flatten the marzipan and sprinkle with the cocoa. Knead until the cocoa is thoroughly combined.
9. Brush the cake lightly with honey. Roll the marzipan and cover the cake, trimming the edges with a sharp knife. Leave on one side.
10. Remove the cabbage leaves carefully. Wash and dry them.
11. Melt the white chocolate in the usual way (page 15). Make an icing bag (page 17), insert the nozzle, and pipe chocolate stamens on to a sheet of greaseproof paper, as shown. Leave on one side.
12. Have 3 bowls ready. Melt the milk and plain chocolates, separately. Mix the 3 chocolates to give 3 shades of brown – pale, medium, and dark.
13. Select 5 outer leaves, 4 centre leaves a little smaller, and 4 inner leaves, smaller still.
14. Lay the outer leaves, underside facing upwards (where the veins are more prominent), on the table. Using a small spoon, coat each leaf carefully with the pale chocolate. Leave on one side to set.
15. Repeat with the centre leaves and medium-brown chocolate, then with the inner leaves and the darkest chocolate.
16. When all the leaves have set, re-coat them, making sure that the previous layer of chocolate is well covered. Leave to set.
17. Rinse your wrists under the cold water tap – to ensure cool hands, otherwise the chocolate will mark or melt. If pieces of leaf tear and remain attached to the chocolate, ease them off with the point of a sharp knife.
18. Coat the centre of the cake with melted chocolate. Leave it until almost set, then position the outer leaves.
19. Position the centre leaves, using melted chocolate to secure, then position the inner leaves, again using chocolate to secure. Pour some chocolate in the centre, leave until almost set, then carefully push in the stamens. Paint a little red food colouring on some of the stamen tips.
20. If the leaves begin to form a 'bloom' before you display or eat the cake, brush them with a light vegetable or nut oil.

Swan Lake

110g (4oz) sunflower margarine
85g (3oz) soft brown sugar
2 eggs
110g (4oz) self-raising flour
30g (1oz) cocoa

335g (12oz) marzipan
30g (1oz) cocoa
Clear honey, mild
110g (4oz) icing sugar
1 egg white
Blue food colouring
approx. 225g (8oz) milk chocolate
approx. 110g (4oz) each of white chocolate
and plain chocolate

200mm (8in.) round sandwich tin
Greaseproof paper
Sheets of white A4 paper
Silicone paper
Ateco (or equivalent) icing nozzle no. 2
14 small geranium leaves

1. To make the chocolate cake, lightly grease and line the tin with greaseproof paper. Preheat the oven to 190°C. (375°F., gas mark 5).
2. Sieve the flour and cocoa in a basin.
3. Beat the sugar and margarine in another basin until pale brown, smooth and creamy.
4. Beat the eggs into the margarine, one at a time, following each with a spoonful of the flour/cocoa mixture. Fold in the remaining flour.
5. Spoon the mixture into the prepared tin. Smooth the surface and place on the centre shelf of the oven for 30–35 minutes, or until firm on top and coming away slightly from the sides of the tin.
6. Leave the cake in the tin for 5–10 minutes, then transfer the cake to a wire tray, first removing the lining paper. Leave until cold.
7. Slice any bumps from the top of the cake, then turn it over.
8. Knead the marzipan and roll it out on a dusted surface. Brush the top of the cake with honey. Lay the marzipan on top and trim round.
9. Flatten the remaining marzipan and sprinkle it with the cocoa. Knead until the cocoa is thoroughly blended. Roll into a long sausage, then roll flat with the rolling pin. Cut a piece to go round the cake with about 2mm (1/10in.) to stand above the top. Brush the cake sides with honey and apply the marzipan.

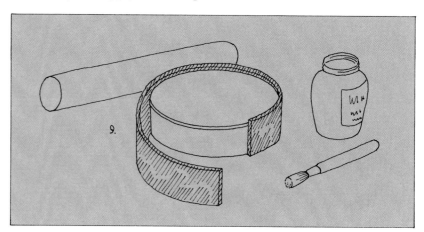

10. Break the egg white on to a saucer. Take as near half of it as possible and slide it into a clean basin. Sprinkle the egg white with icing sugar and beat thoroughly until smooth. Add some more egg white and a little water until the mixture is thick but pourable.
11. Carefully pour the icing into the cake recess. Drop some blue colouring, at intervals, on to the icing, then swirl it around with a skewer. Leave on one side to set.

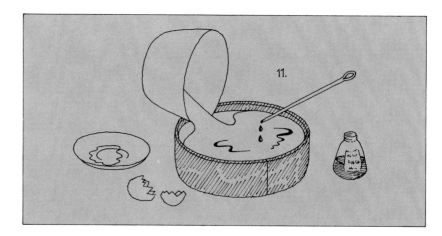

Photograph opposite.
This delicately moulded chocolate swan floats calmly on a lake of icing. The cake base is topped with marzipan, before icing, and is decorated with coated geranium leaves and flower shapes.
The whole glorious confection is a feast for the eyes and taste buds.

12. Trace the swan on to a piece of paper and the wing-pieces on to another. Reverse the tracing and trace the images on to 2 more sheets. You should now have the left-hand and right-hand sides of the swan. Tape the tracings to a table, then tape a sheet of silicone paper over the top of each. Trace the lily petals, well spaced, on to another sheet of paper and cover with silicone as before.

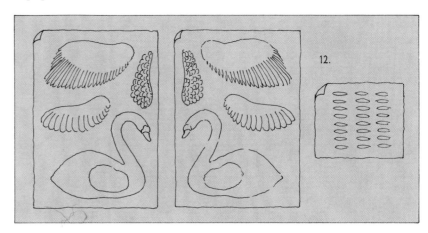

13. Melt the milk chocolate in the usual way (page 15), then remove from heat. Make an icing bag (page 17) and insert the nozzle. Spoon the chocolate into the bag and follow the outline of both swans, omitting the beak area, as shown.

14. Allow the line a few minutes to set, then start to fill in the area, building it up so that the neck and body become full and rounded. When the chocolate is almost set, pull it out in little tufts with a spoon handle, omitting the areas where the wings will be attached, as shown.

15. Melt the plain chocolate. Pipe the outline and feathers of both sets of wing-pieces and the dark area of the beak. Fill in the solid areas of the 4 larger wing pieces. Leave to set.

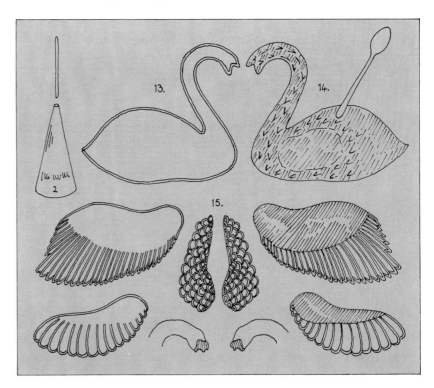

16. Cut the smallest, flattest geranium leaves from the plant, with their stalks, 2 or 3 at a time. Wash and dry them carefully if they have been outside or sprayed with insecticide. Turn them, underside facing upwards, and coat carefully with the melted chocolate. Use a skewer and make sure all little crevices are filled up to the edge. Leave to set.

17. Pipe the petals for 3 lilies, about 10 for each, and fill them in at the same time as piping the outline – so that there is no discernible line around each one. Cut the silicone into squares, each square supporting a petal, then attach 18 squares to a rolling pin, securing them with adhesive tape. Attach those remaining to something with a more acute curve (I used a smaller, child's rolling pin). Leave to set.

18. Re-melt the milk chocolate. Pipe the petals for 3 more lilies, as before.

19. Melt the white chocolate and add some to some of the milk chocolate. Using a skewer, carefully fill in the feathers of the largest wing-pieces. Before the chocolate sets, pipe a line of milk chocolate on top of the paler colour, coming from the start of the feather out towards the tip.

20. Fill in the feathers of the middle wing-pieces with white chocolate, using the pale chocolate (used for the previous wing-pieces) to blend in, as shown in the photograph.

21. Fill in the feathers of the smaller wing-pieces with white chocolate. Pipe and fill in the beak.

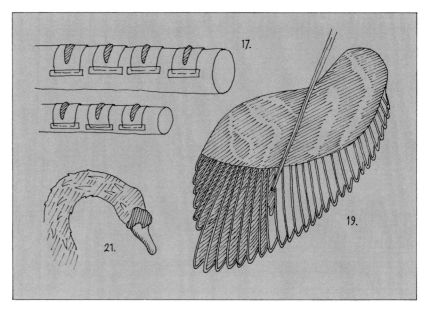

22. Re-melt the plain chocolate. Pipe a squiggly lily stem around the edge of the cake. Attach the lily (geranium) leaves while the stem is still soft. Assemble the lilies on the cake, using melted chocolate to secure the petals in position.

23. Rinse your wrists under the cold water tap – this will ensure cool hands. Handle the chocolate carefully and stick the 2 swan halves together with melted chocolate. Pare away some chocolate at the bottom to allow the swan to stand upright.

24. Attach the large wing-pieces first, using melted chocolate. Attach the middle wing-pieces with enough chocolate to force them out a little. Repeat with the small wing-pieces, again pushing them out a little.

25. Smear some chocolate on the underside of the swan and position it on the cake.

Cakes Buns & Slices

Cakes Buns & Slices

Traditional chocolate cake

170g (6oz) butter
170g (6oz) caster sugar
3 eggs, separated
1 teasp vanilla essence
280g (10oz) plain flour
2 teasp baking powder
2 tblsp cocoa
285ml (½pt) cold water

45g (1½oz) plain chocolate
85g (3oz) butter
200g (7oz) icing sugar

1. Butter and flour two 230mm (9in.) cake tins. Preheat the oven to 180°C. (350°F., gas mark 4).
2. Cream the butter and sugar in a large basin, until the mixture is pale and fluffy.
3. Beat in the egg yolks, one at a time, then the vanilla essence.
4. Sift the flour, baking powder and cocoa into another basin. Fold into the butter mixture alternately with the water. Beat thoroughly after each addition.
5. Whisk the egg whites until soft peaks form, then carefully fold them into the mixture.
6. Divide the mixture equally between the two tins. Bake for 30–35 minutes, or until firm on top and coming away slightly from the sides of the tins.
7. Leave to cool in the tins for a few minutes, then remove and cool on a wire tray.
8. Melt the chocolate in the usual way (page 15).
9. Sieve the icing sugar. Keep a tablespoonful back for the top of the cake.
10. Place the butter in a basin. Cream it and gradually blend in the icing sugar. Pour in the melted chocolate. Beat well, adding a little more sifted icing sugar if required.
11. Sandwich the cakes together with the chocolate butter cream and dust the top of the cake with the remaining icing sugar.
Serves 8–12.

Spiced chocolate squares

200g (7oz) plain chocolate
140g (5oz) butter
225g (8oz) caster sugar
3 eggs, separated
170g (6oz) flour
¼ teasp each of nutmeg,
cinnamon, allspice and cloves
7 tblsp milk
2 teasp finely chopped mixed peel
4 tblsp evaporated milk
1 tblsp golden syrup

1. Grease and line with greaseproof paper a 200mm (8in.) square baking tin. Preheat the oven to 180°C. (350°F., gas mark 4).
2. Melt 85g (3oz) of the chocolate in the usual way (page 15).
3. Cream 110g (4oz) of the butter and 170g (6oz) of the sugar until pale and fluffy. Blend in the egg yolks and melted chocolate.
4. Sieve the flour and spices into a basin, and then add it alternately with the milk, to the creamed mixture. Also add the peel and mix thoroughly.
5. Whisk the egg whites until stiff peaks form. Carefully fold into the mixture.
6. Transfer the mixture to the prepared baking tin. Bake for 30–40 minutes, or until the top is firm and the cake is coming away slightly from the edges of the tin.
7. Leave to cool in the tin for 10 minutes, then remove lining paper and leave to cool on a wire tray.
8. Pour the evaporated milk into a heavy-based pan, on a low heat.
9. Add the golden syrup and remaining butter and sugar. Stir until the butter melts and sugar dissolves.
10. Increase the heat to medium and bring to the boil. Then reduce heat to low and simmer gently, stirring occasionally, for 5 minutes.
11. Remove from heat. Break the remaining chocolate into the mixture and beat until smooth. Refrigerate until the mixture becomes spreadable.
12. Using a palette knife, coat the top of the cake with the icing. Cut into 16 squares.
Makes 16.

Orange chocolate cake

225g (8oz) butter
170g (6oz) caster sugar
225g (8oz) self-raising flour
85g (3oz) cocoa
2 eggs
1 orange
140ml (5fl. oz) buttermilk

170g (6oz) butter
450g (1lb) icing sugar
15g (½oz) cocoa
1½ teasp water
oil of jaffa, or orange flavouring
orange food colour
55g (2oz) grated chocolate

1. Butter and flour two 230mm (8in.) cake tins. Preheat the oven to 180°C. (350°F., gas mark 4).
2. Place the butter and sugar in a basin and cream them until pale and fluffy. Gradually beat in the eggs.
3. Grate the orange finely, taking care not to include the pith. Add it to the mixture. Halve the orange and extract the juice.
4. Add enough orange juice to the buttermilk to make 225ml (8fl. oz).
5. Beat the liquids into the creamed mixture, then gradually fold in the flour and cocoa.
6. Divide the mixture equally between the two tins. Bake for 45 minutes, or until firm on top and coming away slightly from the sides of the tin.
9. Remove and leave to cool in the tins for 5–10 minutes. Turn out on to a wire tray and leave until completely cold.
10. Have ready two basins. Put 85g (3oz) of butter in each. Sift the icing sugar and gradually blend 225g (8oz) into each basin.
11. Sift the cocoa into one basin and blend thoroughly.
12. Blend ¼ teaspoonful of jaffa oil (or orange flavouring) and a few drops of orange food colour into the other mixture.
13. Take one of the cakes and carefully slice any bumps off the top. Turn the cake over and proceed to ice: first, score the surface with a knife, dividing it into 4 sections; then, using a small star nozzle, fill an icing bag (see page 17) with chocolate butter icing and pipe stars in two opposite sections.

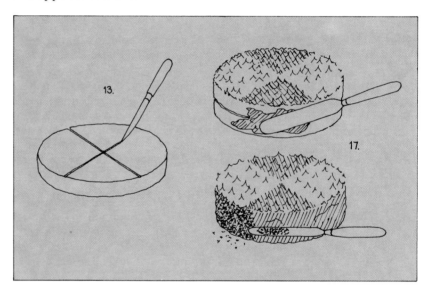

14. Repeat with the orange icing, filling in the other two sections.
15. Mix enough of the two icings together to fill and coat the sides of the cake.
16. Slice any bumps off the top of the other cake. Smear the sliced side with icing and put the iced cake on top.
17. Coat the sides and, with the help of a palette knife, cover with grated chocolate.
18. Using the remaining chocolate and orange icings, pipe the top and bottom edges, as shown, then pipe across the centre, finishing with a double star.
Serves 8–10.

Photograph opposite.
This rich chocolate and orange cake is decorated with piped stars made from butter icing.
Chilled chocolate slab is made from crushed digestive biscuits and chopped hazel nuts. As its name indicates, it is best when it is eaten chilled from the refrigerator.

Black Forest gateau

55g (2oz) softened butter
30g (1oz) caster sugar
55g (2oz) plain flour
30g (1oz) cornflour

110g (4oz) softened butter
110g (4oz) caster sugar
2 medium-sized eggs
85g (3oz) S.R. flour
30g (1oz) cocoa powder
1 teasp vanilla essence

------

1 × 425g (15oz) can black cherries
1 × 425g (15oz) can red cherries
2 tblsp cherry brandy
2 tblsp raspberry jam
285ml (½pt) double cream
140ml (¼pt) single cream
85g (3oz) plain chocolate
12 chocolate shapes (see page 18)

1. Grease and dust with cocoa a 23cm (9in.) cake tin. Preheat the oven to 190°C. (375°F., gas mark 5).
2. To make the shortbread base, cream the 55g (2oz) of butter and the 30g (1oz) of sugar until the mixture is pale and fluffy.
3. Sieve the flour and cornflour together and gradually knead them into the butter to form a smooth dough.
4. Press the dough into the cake tin and smooth the top with a palette knife. Prick the surface all over with a fork.
5. Bake on the upper middle shelf for 20 minutes or until pale golden brown.
6. Remove from the oven and leave to cool on a wire tray.
7. Clean the cake tin, re-grease it, line the bottom with greaseproof paper and dust the sides with cocoa.
8. To make the cake, cream the butter and sugar until pale and fluffy. Beat the eggs and add them to the butter a little at a time. Sieve the flour and cocoa together and gradually fold in.
9. Add the vanilla essence; then spread the mixture evenly in the prepared cake tin.
10. Bake in the oven at the same temperature for 20–25 minutes until cooked and springy to the touch.
11. Remove from the tin and leave to cool on a wire tray.
12. Drain the two tins of cherries and add the cherry brandy to the juice. Remove the stones from the cherries.
13. Cut the cake in half and moisten each half with the juice.
14. Place the shortbread on a flat plate. Spread one half of the cake with a layer of cream and, reserving 12 cherries for decoration, evenly scatter the remaining cherries over the cream.
15. Place the other half of the cake on top and lift the whole on to the shortbread base.
16. Carefully cover the whole cake with cream, reserving enough to pipe 12 whirls all around the top.
17. Grate the chocolate, and carefully coat the sides. Pipe the whirls around the top edge.
18. Place alternate black and red cherries on top of each whirl, and complete by inserting a chocolate shape between each cherry.
Serves 8.

Photograph opposite.
Black Forest gateau is a sumptuously rich confection, flavoured with Cherry Brandy, and is the ideal dessert for that special dinner party.
A chocolate sponge cake sits upon a shortbread base and is filled with cherries and cream. It is decorated with grated chocolate, piped cream and cherries.

Chilled chocolate slab

170g (6oz) butter
170g (6oz) plain chocolate
170g (6oz) chopped hazelnuts
2 eggs
170g (6oz) wholemeal digestive biscuits

1. Lightly butter a 130mm (5in.) square baking tin.
2. Chop the butter and place it in a heavy-based pan, on a low heat.
3. Break the chocolate into pieces and add it to the butter. When the two have melted stir in the chopped nuts and mix thoroughly.
4. Beat the eggs thoroughly and add them to the mixture. Remove from heat.
5. Chop the biscuits into small pieces and stir them into the mixture.
6. Spoon the mixture into the tin, spreading it evenly with the back of a spoon. Cover with foil and refrigerate for 24 hours.
7. Remove 15 minutes before serving and cut into slices.
Serves 10–20.

Chocolate roulade

170g (6oz) plain chocolate
1 tblsp water
2 eggs, separated
1 tblsp Amaretto or Grand Marnier

------

5 large eggs, separated
110g (4oz) caster sugar
55g (2oz) cocoa

Icing sugar for dusting
225ml (8fl. oz) double cream

1. Lightly oil a 300mm × 180mm × 25mm (12in. × 7in. × 1in.) Swiss roll tin. Line the base and sides with greaseproof paper. Oil the paper lightly.
2. Melt the chocolate in the usual way (page 15), adding the tablespoonful of water. Remove from heat when melted.
3. Beat the two egg yolks, then beat them into the chocolate. Stir in the liqueur.
4. Whisk the egg whites until stiff peaks form. Fold them into the chocolate, carefully but thoroughly. Cover and refrigerate until the cake is ready. Preheat the oven to 180°C. (350°F., gas mark 4).
5. Whisk the 5 egg yolks and sugar until thick and creamy. Sift and fold in the cocoa.
6. Whisk the egg whites, in another basin, until stiff peaks form. Again carefully, but thoroughly, fold the whites into the chocolate.
7. Turn the mixture into the tin and spread it evenly. Bake on the centre shelf for 15 minutes, or until just cooked.
8. Wet a tea towel, squeeze it out and cover the tin with it until the cake is cold.
9. Dust a sheet of greaseproof paper liberally with the icing sugar, turn the cake on to it and peel away the lining paper.
10. Spread the chocolate over the cake. Lightly beat the cream and spread it over the chocolate.
11. Roll the roulade, pulling the greaseproof paper up to help push the roll along. Leave it to rest on the seam. Carefully transfer to a serving plate.
Serves 6–8.

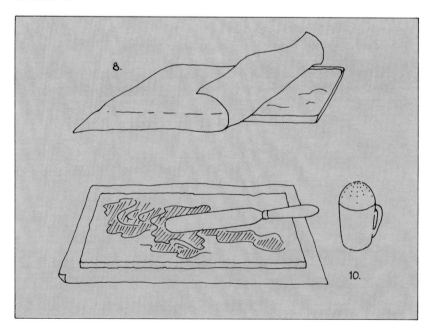

Chocolate ginger slices

200g (7oz) self-raising flour
30g (1oz) cocoa
¼ teasp salt
2 teasp ground ginger
85g (3oz) butter
55g (2oz) soft brown sugar
3 tblsp golden syrup
2 eggs
Milk
55g (2oz) crystallised ginger

15g (½oz) butter
45g (1½oz) plain chocolate
200g (7oz) icing sugar
2 tblsp milk

55g (2oz) milk chocolate
Few drops vegetable oil

1. Butter and line with greaseproof paper a 180mm (7in.) square baking tin. Cut the sides of the paper large enough to come above the sides of the tin. Preheat the oven to 180°C. (350°F., gas mark 4).
2. Sieve the flour, cocoa, salt and ginger into a basin.
3. Place the butter in a heavy-based pan, on a low heat. Add the sugar and syrup. When the butter has melted and the sugar dissolved, add to the flour mixture and mix thoroughly.
4. Beat the eggs in a measuring jug and add sufficient milk to make 140ml (¼pt). Add this to the other ingredients. Mix well.
5. Keep 12 pieces of ginger for decoration. Chop the remainder and add them to the mixture. Blend all the ingredients thoroughly.
6. Pour the mixture into the prepared tin and bake on the centre shelf for about 45 minutes, or until firm on top and coming away slightly from the sides of the tin.
7. Leave it to cool in the tin, then remove, keeping the lining paper intact. Stand it on a wire tray.
8. Break the plain chocolate and place it with the butter in a heavy-based pan, on a low heat. When melted, sift the icing sugar into the pan, stirring continuously. Stir in the milk.
9. Place the pan in a bowl of iced water and beat the mixture until a spreading consistency is reached.
10. Spread the icing over the cake. When it is firm, remove the lining paper.
11. Melt the milk chocolate in the usual way (page 15), stirring in the oil.
12. Make an icing bag (page 17), fill it with the melted chocolate and snip the end.
13. Pipe divisions on the cake, 5 vertical lines and 1 horizontal, dividing the cake into 12. Pipe zigzag lines on each section, then decorate with a piece of ginger.
Makes 12.

Chocolate butterfly cakes

110g (4oz) butter
110g (4oz) caster sugar
85g (3oz) self-raising flour
30g (1oz) cocoa
2 eggs
200g (7oz) whipping cream
Icing sugar for dusting

1. Arrange 12 bun cases in a tray of deep patty tins. Preheat the oven to 180°C. (350°F., gas mark 4).
2. Beat the butter and sugar until pale and fluffy.
3. Sift the flour and cocoa into a basin. Beat the two eggs thoroughly in a small bowl.
4. Beat the eggs and a tablespoonful of flour and cocoa into the butter alternately, then fold in any remaining flour.
5. Divide the mixture between the bun cases and bake on the centre shelf for about 20 minutes, or until firm to the touch.
6. When the cakes are cold, slice the tops off, then cut each slice in half.
7. Whip the cream. Fill an icing bag (with a large star nozzle) and pipe a star on each cake. Position 2 pieces of sponge, like butterfly wings, in the cream.
8. Dust the cakes with icing sugar.
Makes 12.

Chocolate profiteroles

140ml (¼pt) water
55g (2oz) butter
70g (2½oz) plain flour
2 eggs

170ml (6fl. oz) double cream

140g (5oz) plain chocolate
1 tblsp golden syrup
140ml (¼pt) single cream

1. Butter and lightly flour a baking sheet. Preheat the oven to 200°C. (400°F., gas mark 6). Sieve the flour into a dish.
2. Pour the water into a heavy-based pan, on a low heat. Chop the butter and add it to the water. When the butter has melted, increase the heat to medium and bring the mixture to boiling point.
3. Remove from heat and immediately pour in all the flour. Beat thoroughly until the mixture leaves the sides of the pan clean.
4. Beat the eggs together, then add a little at a time to the pan, beating vigorously after each addition. The mixture should become very glossy.
5. Spoon the mixture into an icing bag fitted with a 12mm (½in.) plain nozzle. Pipe small rounds (about 24) on to the prepared baking sheet keeping them well apart.
6. Bake for 15 minutes, then reduce heat to 180°C. (350°F., gas mark 4) for a further 10 minutes, or until golden brown.
7. Make a slit in the side of each profiterole to let out the steam. Leave to cool on a wire tray.
8. Whip the cream, spoon it into the icing bag and pipe into each cavity.
9. Pile the profiteroles on to a serving dish in the form of a pyramid.
10. Melt the chocolate in the usual way (page 15). When melted, remove from heat and mix in the syrup. Beat in the cream. Pour the sauce into a jug.
11. Starting with the bottom row of profiteroles, pour the sauce around the pyramid, eventually reaching the top.
Makes 20–24.

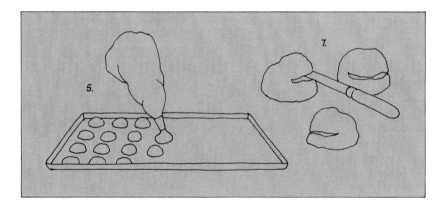

Chocolate éclairs

140ml (¼pt) cold water
55g (2oz) butter
70g (2½oz) plain flour
2 eggs

170ml (6fl. oz) double cream

110g (4oz) plain chocolate
2 tblsp single cream

1. Butter and lightly flour a baking sheet. Preheat the oven to 200°C. (400°F., gas mark 6).
2. To make the choux pastry, follow instructions 2 to 5 for profiteroles in the previous recipe.
3. Spoon the mixture into an icing bag fitted with a 20mm (¾in.) plain nozzle. Pipe 10 strips on to the prepared baking sheet 75mm (3in.) long.
4. Bake for 10 minutes, then reduce the heat to 190°C. (375°F., gas mark 5) and bake for a further 10 minutes, or until golden brown.
5. Make a slit down the side of each éclair and leave to cool on a wire tray.
6. Whip the cream, then fill the piping bag, fitted with a 12mm (½in.) plain nozzle, and pipe the cream into each éclair.
7. Melt the chocolate in the usual way (page 15). When melted remove from heat and beat in the cream.
8. Carefully dip the surface of each éclair into the chocolate. Then place on a wire tray until set.
Makes 8–10.

Sachertorte

170g (6oz) plain chocolate
110g (4oz) butter
8 eggs, separated
1 teasp vanilla essence
2 egg whites
pinch of salt
170g (6oz) caster sugar
110g (4oz) plain flour

225g (8oz) apricot jam

170g (6oz) double cream
1 teasp golden syrup
85g (3oz) plain chocolate
225g (8oz) caster sugar
1 egg
1 teasp vanilla essence

This 'lighter than air' torte was first created in 1832 and has become one of Vienna's most acclaimed cakes. At one stage it was the issue of a celebrated court case which produced more excitement in Vienna and used more newspaper space than a minor war.

1. Grease and line with greaseproof paper two 230mm (9in.) cake tins. Preheat the oven to 180°C. (350°F., gas mark 4).
2. Melt the chocolate in the usual way (page 15). Chop and add the butter.
3. Put the egg yolks into a basin and break them up with a fork. Beat in the melted chocolate and butter, then the vanilla essence.
4. Whisk the 10 egg whites, with the salt, until they begin to foam. Gradually beat in the sugar. Continue whisking until stiff peaks form.
5. Mix one-third of the whites into the chocolate mixture, then pour the chocolate over the remaining egg whites.
6. Sift the flour and very carefully fold it into the mixture. Continue until no trace of egg white can be seen, but do not over-fold.
7. Divide the mixture between the two tins and bake in the centre of the oven until the cakes are puffed and dry, and a toothpick stuck into the centre comes out dry.
8. Turn the cakes on to a wire rack and remove the paper lining. Leave to cool.
9. Place the cream and syrup in a heavy-based pan, on a low heat. Break the chocolate into the cream and add the sugar. Stir the mixture continuously with a wooden spoon and cook until the chocolate melts and the sugar dissolves.
10. Raise to a medium heat and cook without stirring for 5 minutes, or until a blob of mixture dropped into a cup of cold water forms a soft ball. Reduce heat.
11. Beat the egg lightly in a small basin. Stir in 3 tablespoonfuls of the chocolate mixture. Pour this into the pan and mix thoroughly.
12. Stir continuously on a low heat for 3–4 minutes, or until the mixture thickly coats the back of the spoon. Remove from heat and stir in the vanilla essence. Leave to cool at room temperature.
13. When the cakes are cold, sieve the jam and sandwich the two together.
14. Position the wire tray (with the cake on) over a baking sheet and pour the glaze evenly over, smoothing it with a palette knife.
15. When the glaze ceases to drip, transfer the cake, with the help of a fish slice and palette knife, to a plate and refrigerate for 3 hours.
16. Remove from refrigerator 30 minutes before serving.
Serves 6–8.

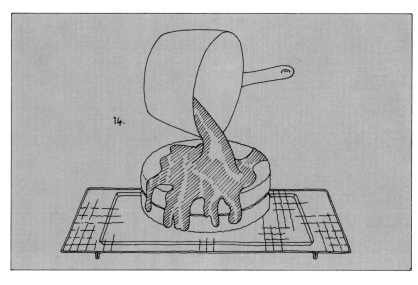

Chocolate almond patties

225g (8oz) plain flour
55g (2oz) caster sugar
½ teasp salt
1 heaped tblsp ground almonds
140g (5oz) butter
1 egg yolk

170g (6oz) plain chocolate
2 tblsp Amaretto
2 egg yolks
285ml (½pt) double cream

170ml (6fl. oz) whipping cream
55g–85g (2oz–3oz) unblanched almonds

1. Sift the flour and salt into a basin. Mix in the sugar and almonds.
2. Chop the butter. Make a well in the centre of the flour and drop in the butter and egg yolk.
3. Using fingertips, incorporate all the ingredients. Form into a ball, wrap in clingfilm and refrigerate for an hour. Preheat the oven to 190°C. (375°F., gas mark 5).
4. Roll the pastry on a lightly floured surface and cut 12 × 75mm (3in.) circles. Place the circles in a tray of patty tins and prick each one several times with a fork.
5. Bake until golden brown, about 15 minutes. Leave to cool in the tin.
6. Melt the chocolate in the usual way (page 15). When it is melted remove from heat and stir in the Amaretto. Allow to cool a little, then beat in the egg yolks. Beat until the mixture cools completely.
7. Whip the cream and fold it into the mixture. Spoon into each patty case. Refrigerate until the mixture firms.
8. Whip the whipping cream until it is stiff. Fill an icing bag, fitted with a star nozzle, and pipe a star on each patty. Decorate each with 2 or 3 almonds.
Makes 12.

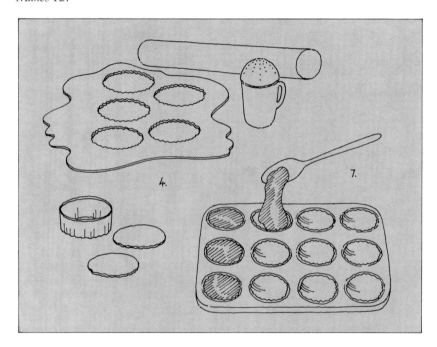

Brownies

110g (4oz) plain chocolate
85g (3oz) butter, chopped
3 eggs
¼ teasp salt
170g (6oz) caster sugar
85g (3oz) self-raising flour
110g (4oz) chopped walnuts

1. Butter and line with greaseproof paper a 200mm (8in.) square baking tin. Preheat the oven to 180°C, (350°F., gas mark 4).
2. Melt the chocolate in the usual way (page 15). Add the butter. When both have melted, remove from heat.
3. Break the eggs into a basin. Add the salt and whisk until fluffy. Add the sugar. Whisk until thoroughly blended.
4. Stir the chocolate mixture into the eggs.
5. Sift the flour and gradually add it to the mixture. Add the walnuts. Stir again to ensure thorough combination of all ingredients. Pour into the prepared tin and smooth the surface.
6. Bake on the centre shelf for about 25 minutes, or until firm to the touch.
7. Leave to cool in the tin. Then remove lining paper and cut into 16 squares.
Makes 16.

Chocolate Florentine slices

110g (4oz) butter
85g (3oz) caster sugar
2 eggs
85g (3oz) self-raising flour
½ teasp baking powder
30g (1oz) cocoa

110g (4oz) marzipan

85g (3oz) butter
55g (2oz) caster sugar
55g (2oz) glacé cherries
30g (1oz) candied peel
30g (1oz) angelica
110g (4oz) flaked almonds

85g (3oz) plain chocolate

1. Butter and line a 180mm × 280mm (7in. × 11in.) baking tin. Preheat the oven to 180°C. (350°F., gas mark 4).
2. Chop the butter into a basin. Add the sugar and beat until the mixture is pale and fluffy.
3. Beat the eggs in a cup.
4. Sift the flour, baking powder and cocoa in another basin. Mix the eggs and flour alternately into the butter. Pour the mixture into the prepared tin and smooth the surface with a palette knife.
5. Grate the marzipan evenly over the surface. Bake on the centre shelf for 20–25 minutes.
Make the topping while the cake is baking:
6. Chop the cherries into quarters. Chop the candied peel, angelica and almonds.
7. Chop the butter into a heavy-based pan. Add the sugar and put on a low heat until the butter melts and sugar dissolves.
8. Bring the mixture to boil, then stir in the cherries, peel, angelica and almonds. Remove from heat and leave to cool.
9. Grate the chocolate. After 20–25 minutes baking remove the cake and, while still hot, sprinkle the chocolate over the marzipan.
10. Spoon the topping evenly over the chocolate and return to the oven for a further 10 minutes.
11. Leave the cake to cool in the tin for 5 minutes, then remove and transfer to a wire tray. When it is cold, cut into 18 bars.
Makes 18.

Delicious florentine slices have a chocolate and marzipan base, cut into slices. When cold each slice is topped with chopped cherries, candied peel, angelica and almonds.

Biscuits & Bars

Biscuits & Bars

Florentines

Rice paper
2 tblsp golden syrup
55g (2oz) butter
55g (2oz) soft brown sugar
55g (2oz) nibbed almonds
30g (1oz) glacé cherries
30g (1oz) raisins
Rind of 1 orange, grated
45g (1½oz) plain flour

170g (6oz) plain chocolate

1. Cover 2 baking trays with rice paper. Preheat the oven to 180°C. (350°F., gas mark 4).
2. Put the syrup, butter (chopped) and sugar in a heavy-based pan, on a low heat.
3. Chop the glacé cherries and raisins.
4. When the butter has melted and the sugar dissolved, add the almonds, cherries, raisins and peel. Mix thoroughly.
5. Sieve the flour into the pan and stir well. Remove from heat.
6. Place teaspoonfuls of the mixture, well apart, on the baking sheets and bake on the centre shelves for 8–10 minutes, or until golden and well spread.
7. Leave to cool slightly on the trays, then remove and cut away the excess rice paper. Leave on a wire tray, with the rice paper facing upwards, until completely cold.
8. Melt the chocolate in the usual way (page 15). When melted spread over the rice paper. Mark zigzag lines with a fork when the chocolate is almost set.
Makes 16–18.

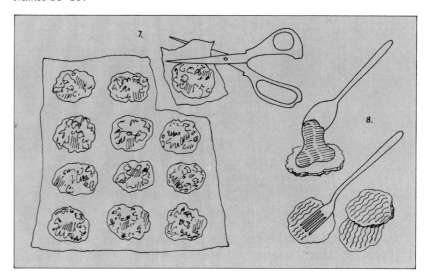

Chocolate hearts

170g (6oz) butter
85g (3oz) caster sugar
170g (6oz) plain flour
30g (1oz) cocoa
55g (2oz) ground almonds

170g (6oz) plain chocolate
55g (2oz) blanched almonds

45g (1½oz) butter
110g (4oz) icing sugar
1 tblsp cocoa
2 tblsp milk

1. Butter and flour 2 baking trays.
2. Chop the butter into a basin. Add the sugar and cream together until light and fluffy.
3. Sieve the flour and cocoa in another basin. Mix in the ground almonds. Gradually beat these dry ingredients into the butter to give a soft dough. Cover and refrigerate for 15 minutes. Preheat the oven to 160°C. (325°F., gas mark 3).
4. Roll the dough on a lightly floured surface. Using a heart-shaped cutter, cut the biscuits and place them on the trays. Bake on the centre shelves for 15 minutes.
5. Leave to cool slightly on the trays, then transfer to a wire tray and leave until cold.
6. Melt the chocolate in the usual way (page 15). Carefully dip the top of each biscuit in the chocolate, top with an almond and leave to set on the wire tray.

7. Place the butter in a basin. Sieve the icing sugar and cocoa over the butter, then add the milk. Beat until all the ingredients are thoroughly combined.

8. Make an icing bag (page 1⁻), insert a small star nozzle, and pipe the icing around the edge of each heart.

Makes 22–24.

Chocolate ginger rings

70g (2½oz) plain flour
55g (2oz) butter
15g (½oz) cocoa
30g (1oz) caster sugar
½ level teasp ground ginger
1 egg yolk

110g (4oz) icing sugar
½ teasp ground ginger
1 tblsp water

55g (2oz) plain chocolate

1. Butter and flour 2 baking trays. Preheat the oven to 180°C. (350°F., gas mark 4).

2. Sieve the flour into a basin. Chop the butter into the flour. Using fingertips, rub the two together until the mixture resembles fine breadcrumbs.

3. Sieve the cocoa into the mixture. Add the sugar and ground ginger, then mix all the ingredients thoroughly.

4. Add the egg yolk and mix to a smooth dough. Knead lightly.

5. Roll the dough on a lightly floured surface. Using a 60mm (2½in.) plain cutter, cut out the biscuits. Cut out the centres with a 25mm (1in.) plain cutter.

6. Place the biscuits on the prepared trays and bake on the middle shelves for 12–15 minutes.

7. Leave the biscuits to cool on the trays for a few minutes, then transfer them to a wire tray.

8. Finely grate the chocolate on to a saucer and refrigerate.

9. Sieve the icing sugar and ginger into a basin. Add the water, a little at a time, until the icing is smooth and thick.

10. Using a small coffee spoon, carefully coat the top of each biscuit, then sprinkle the grated chocolate on top.

Makes 20–25.

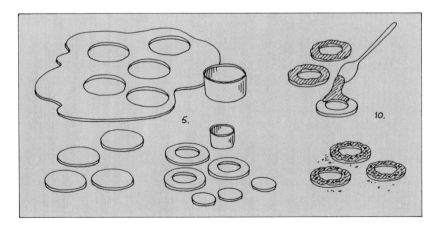

Chocolate walnut bars

100g (3½oz) butter
2 tblsp water
55g (2oz) caster sugar
225g (8oz) finely chopped walnuts

140g (5oz) self-raising flour
15g (½oz) cocoa
pinch of salt
70g (2½oz) butter
1 egg
Fine-shred marmalade

70g (2½oz) plain chocolate

1. Butter a 230mm × 330mm (9in. × 13in.) Swiss roll tin. Preheat the oven to 180°C. (350°F., gas mark 4).
2. Chop the butter into a heavy-based pan, and put it on a low heat. Add the water and sugar. Stir until the butter has melted and the sugar dissolved. Increase the heat to medium and bring the mixture to boil. Remove from heat and leave until cool.
3. Sieve the flour, cocoa and salt into a basin. Chop the butter into the basin and, using fingertips, rub it into the dry ingredients until the mixture resembles fine breadcrumbs.
4. Beat the egg. Add it to the flour and mix to form a soft dough. Turn on to a lightly floured surface, knead lightly, then roll out and fit into the baking tin.
5. Warm the marmalade and spread a film over the pastry.
6. Add the chopped walnuts to the cooled butter. Mix well, then spread over the marmalade. Bake on the middle shelf for 30 minutes.
7. Leave to cool slightly, then cut into 16 bars and place on a wire tray. Refrigerate for 30 minutes.
8. Melt the chocolate in the usual way (page 15). Make an icing bag (see page 17), spoon in the mixture, snip the point off the bag and drizzle the chocolate over each bar.
Makes 16.

Chocolate flapjacks

110g (4oz) butter
55g (2oz) plain chocolate
1 tblsp golden syrup
85g (3oz) soft brown sugar
85g (3oz) cornflakes
55g (2oz) self-raising flour
55g (2oz) rolled oats

1. Generously butter a Swiss roll tin. Preheat the oven to 190°C. (375°F., gas mark 5).
2. Chop the butter into a heavy-based pan, on a low heat. Break the chocolate into pieces and add it to the butter. Add the golden syrup and sugar.
3. Put the cornflakes into a strong polythene bag and crush them with a rolling pin.
4. When the butter and chocolate have melted and the sugar is dissolved, stir thoroughly and remove from heat.

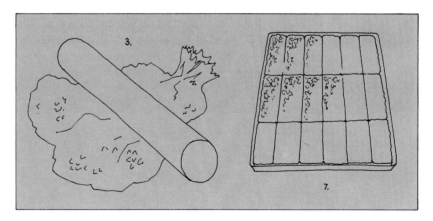

5. Put the cornflakes, flour and oats into a large basin. Mix, then make a well in the centre. Pour in the melted ingredients and blend thoroughly.
6. Press the mixture into the tin and bake on the centre shelf for 15–20 minutes.
7. Cut into fingers while still hot in the tin. Leave to cool, then remove and leave on a wire tray until cold.
Makes 18–21.

Chocolate raisin bars

225g (8oz) plain chocolate
3 eggs
110g (4oz) caster sugar
170g (6oz) desiccated coconut
110g (4oz) seedless raisins

1. Line a 180mm × 280mm × 25mm (7in. × 11in. × 1in.) baking tin with foil. Brush it lightly with oil.
2. Melt the chocolate in the usual way (page 15). Pour it evenly into the lined tin and refrigerate until set, about 30 minutes. Preheat the oven to 180°C. (350°F., gas mark 4).
3. Beat the eggs and sugar until thoroughly blended. Fold in the coconut and raisins. Mix thoroughly.
4. Spread the mixture evenly over the chocolate. Bake on the centre shelf for 30 minutes.
5. Leave to cool in the tin, then place the tin in the refrigerator for about 30 minutes.
6. Turn the slab out of the tin and cut into bars.
Makes 18–21.

Chocolate hazelnut cookies

55g (2oz) butter
55g (2oz) soft brown sugar
55g (2oz) chopped hazelnuts
85g (3oz) self-raising flour

85g (3oz) milk chocolate

1. Butter and flour 2 baking sheets. Preheat the oven to 180°C. (350°F., gas mark 4).
2. Chop the butter into a basin. Add the sugar and mix to a smooth cream consistency. Stir in the hazelnuts.
3. Sieve the flour into the mixture and blend to form a soft dough.
4. Using damp hands, form the dough into small round balls. Position 8 on each tray, well apart, then flatten with the heel of your thumb. Bake on the centre shelves for 10–12 minutes.
5. Leave to cool on the sheets for a few minutes, then transfer to a wire tray. Leave until cold.
6. Melt the chocolate in the usual way (page 15). Dip one third of each cookie into the chocolate, then leave to set on the wire tray.
7. Remelt the chocolate and, holding the uncoated edges of each cookie, dip the opposite third. Leave on the wire tray to set.
Makes 12–15.

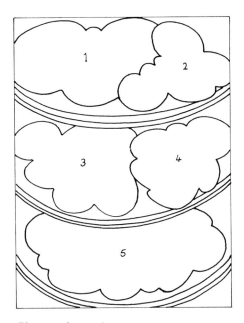

Photograph opposite.
A selection of chocolate biscuits to grace your tea-table. The diagram on this page indicates each respective recipe.
1. Chocolate creams. 2. Chocolate almond macaroons. 3. Hazelnut cookies. 4. Chocolate ginger rings. 5. Chip biscuits.

Digestive biscuits

110g (4oz) wholewheat flour
½ teasp baking powder
55g (2oz) soft brown sugar
55g (2oz) medium oatmeal
55g (2oz) butter
1 tblsp milk

85g (3oz) plain chocolate

1. Butter and lightly flour a baking sheet. Preheat the oven to 180°C. (350°F., gas mark 4).
2. Sieve the flour and baking powder into a basin. Stir in the sugar and oatmeal.
3. Chop the butter into the basin. Using fingertips, rub the butter into the dry ingredients until it resembles breadcrumbs. Add the milk and bind the ingredients to a soft dough.
4. Roll on to a lightly floured surface, to a thickness just less than 6mm (¼in.). Using a plain 60mm (2½in.) cutter, cut into rounds. Re-roll the trimmings and repeat. Transfer the rounds to the prepared baking sheet. Prick each round 4 times with a fork. Bake on the centre shelf for 15–20 minutes.
5. Leave to cool for a few minutes on the sheet, then transfer to a wire tray.
6. Melt the chocolate in the usual way (page 15). Remove from heat and spread over the underside of each biscuit. When almost set mark lines with a palette knife or fork.
Makes 9–11.

Chocolate creams

85g (3oz) butter
45g (1½oz) soft brown sugar
110g (4oz) plain flour
30g (1oz) cocoa

55g (2oz) plain chocolate
45g (1½oz) milk chocolate

1. Butter and lightly flour 2 baking sheets. Preheat the oven to 160°C. (325°F., gas mark 3).
2. Chop the butter into a basin. Add the sugar, then beat until well combined.
3. Sieve the flour and cocoa together and gradually fold them into the butter. Mix until the ingredients bind together, then turn on to a floured surface. Roll out thinly and cut into rounds using a 60mm (2½in.) fluted cutter. Using a 25mm (1in.) cutter, cut the centres from half the number of rounds.
4. Gather the trimmings, roll and repeat until all the dough has been used. Place the rounds on the prepared baking sheets and bake on the centre shelves for 20 minutes.
5. Leave to cool on the sheets.
6. Melt the two chocolates, separately, in the usual way (page 15). Remove from heat and leave to cool, then sandwich the plain and holed biscuits together with a layer of plain chocolate.
7. Make a piping bag (see page 17). Fit it with a small plain nozzle, pipe lines over the top of the biscuits and a row of dots around the edge of the hole.
Makes 12–14.

Chip biscuits

110g (4oz) butter
55g (2oz) soft brown sugar
1 egg
140g (5oz) self-raising flour
170g (6oz) plain chocolate

1. Butter and lightly flour 3 baking sheets. Preheat the oven to 180°C. (350F., gas mark 4).
2. Chop the butter into a basin. Add the sugar and cream together until they are thoroughly blended and the sugar grains can no longer be felt.
3. Beat the egg into the butter, then sieve the flour and fold it in. Mix all the ingredients thoroughly.
4. Chop the chocolate finely and stir it into the mixture. Drop 9 teaspoonsful on to each baking sheet. Bake on the centre shelves for 15–20 minutes, or until golden brown.
5. Leave to cool on the sheets for 5 minutes, then transfer to a wire tray and leave until cold.
Makes 18–20.

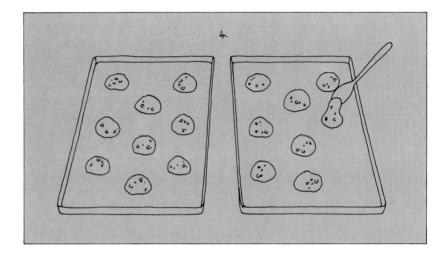

Chocolate peanut bars

55g (2oz) butter
2 tblsp clear honey
110g (4oz) plain chocolate
55g (2oz) salted peanuts
55g (2oz) bran flakes

1. Butter and line with greaseproof paper a shallow 150mm (6in.) square baking tin.
2. Chop the butter into a heavy-based pan, on a low heat. Add the honey. Break the chocolate into pieces and add them to the pan. Stir occasionally until melted.
3. Put the peanuts and bran into 2 separate polythene bags. Crush them with a rolling pin. Stir both in to the melted ingredients. Mix thoroughly.
4. Turn the mixture into the prepared tin. Smooth the surface and refrigerate until set.
5. Cut 5 horizontal lines, and a vertical line down the centre, to make 10 bars. To make smaller bars cut 2 vertical lines.
Makes 18–21.

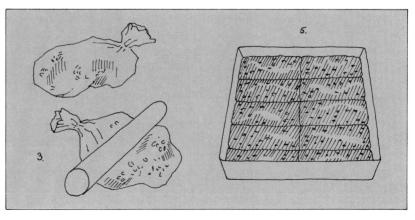

Chocolate almond macaroons

2 large egg whites
85g (3oz) caster sugar
110g (4oz) ground almonds
1 teasp ground rice
1 teasp cocoa
¼ teasp almond essence

85g (3oz) plain chocolate
55g (2oz) whole blanched almonds

1. Butter and lightly flour 2 baking sheets. Preheat the oven to 160°C. (325°F., gas mark 3).
2. Whisk the egg whites until soft peaks form. Whisk the sugar in, a little at a time, and continue to whisk until the mixture is glossy and thick.
3. Fold in the almonds, rice and cocoa. Stir in the essence.
4. Spoon the mixture into a large icing bag fitted with a 25mm (1in.) plain nozzle. Pipe 8 blobs on to each baking sheet. Bake on the middle shelves for 15–20 minutes.
5. Leave to cool on the baking sheets for a few minutes, then transfer to a wire tray. Leave until cold.
6. Melt the chocolate in the usual way (page 15). Remove from heat and leave to cool.
7. Make an icing bag (see page 17), pour in the cooled chocolate, then snip the point off the bag. Pipe a continuous circle starting around the edge of the macaroon and ending with a blob in the middle. Press an almond into the blob. Continue with the remaining macaroons. Leave the chocolate to set before serving.
Makes 20–22.

Lemon chocolate fingers

170g (6oz) butter
30g (1oz) icing sugar
110g (4oz) self-raising flour
30g (1oz) cornflour
30g (1oz) cocoa
3 drops lemon essence

------

lemon curd

85g (3oz) plain chocolate

1. Butter and lightly flour 2 baking sheets. Preheat the oven to 180°C. (350°F., gas mark 4).
2. Chop the butter into a basin. Sieve the icing sugar over the butter, then cream together until pale.
3. In another basin sieve the two flours and cocoa. Mix well, then gradually beat into the butter. Add the essence and continue to beat until the mixture becomes fluid enough to pipe.
4. Spoon the mixture into a large piping bag fitted with a 12mm (½in.) star nozzle. Pipe the mixture into fingers 60mm (2½in.) long on to the prepared baking sheets. Bake on the centre shelves for 20–25 minutes.
5. Leave to cool on the sheets before transferring to a wire tray.
6. Melt the chocolate in the usual way (page 15). Dip both ends of each finger into the chocolate and then leave to set on the wire tray.
Makes 10.

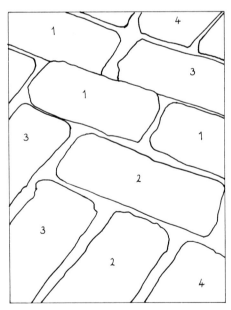

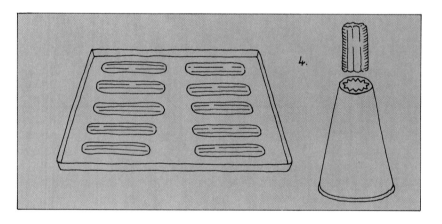

Photograph opposite.
A selection of chocolate bars. The diagram on this page indicates each respective recipe.
1. Chocolate raisin bars. 2. Chocolate walnut bars. 3. Peanut bars. 4. Chocolate cherry bars.

Cherry chocolate bars

100g (3½oz) butter
55g (2oz) soft brown sugar
1 egg
85g (3oz) rolled oats
55g (2oz) self-raising flour
30g (1oz) cocoa
110g (4oz) glacé cherries
85g (3oz) plain chocolate

1. Butter and line with greaseproof paper a 180mm × 280mm (7in. × 11in) Swiss roll tin. Preheat the oven to 180°C. (350°F., gas mark 4).
2. Chop the butter into a basin. Add the sugar and beat until well combined and the sugar grains can no longer be felt.
3. Add the egg and beat to a smooth consistency.
4. Stir in the rolled oats. Sieve the flour and cocoa together and fold them into the mixture. Chop the cherries and fold them in.
5. Chop the chocolate, add it to the basin, then combine all the ingredients thoroughly, adding a little milk if required.
6. Turn the mixture into the prepared tin, smoothing the surface. Bake on the centre shelf for 25 minutes.
7. Leave to cool in the tin before cutting into bars.
Makes 18–21.

Iced chocolate bars

85g (3oz) butter, softened
55g (2oz) lard, softened
55g (2oz) caster sugar
170g (6oz) plain flour
30g (1oz) cocoa powder
55g (2oz) fresh breadcrumbs, toasted
1 teasp vanilla essence

Icing

340g (12oz) icing sugar
55g (2oz) cocoa powder

1. Lightly grease a 20cm × 30cm (8in. × 12in.) Swiss roll tin.
2. Cream together the butter and lard, then beat in the caster sugar till all is light and fluffy.
3. Sieve together the flour and cocoa, and fold into the creamed mixture.
4. Add the breadcrumbs and vanilla essence. Stir until all the ingredients are combined.
5. Spread the mixture evenly in the Swiss roll tin. Bake in a moderate oven, 180°C. (350°F., gas mark 4), for 20 minutes.
6. Divide into 24 pieces and allow to cool in the baking tin.
7. Sieve the icing sugar and cocoa.
8. Carefully add sufficient water to make a spreading consistency.
9. Pour the icing all over the biscuits using a palette knife to spread it evenly.
10. Lift each biscuit on to a wire tray and allow the icing to set. Trim carefully with a sharp knife to give even edges.
Makes 24.

Hot Puddings

Hot Puddings

Chocolate orange pudding

1 large orange
110g (4oz) butter
110g (4oz) caster sugar
4 level tblsp cocoa
2 large eggs
140g (5oz) self-raising flour

1. Butter a 1½pt pudding basin.
2. Finely grate the orange. Cut it in half and squeeze out the juice. Put both to one side.
3. Cream the butter and sugar until it is pale and fluffy.
4. Pour 2 tablespoonfuls of juice into a pan. Add the cocoa. Heat gently and stir until smooth and creamy. Remove from heat and beat into the butter.
5. Beat the eggs lightly, then gradually add them to the butter mixture.
6. Sift the flour and fold it in. Mix to a soft dropping consistency, adding more orange juice if required. Add the orange peel.
7. Spoon the mixture into the basin. Cover the basin with double greaseproof paper and secure it with string. Steam the pudding for 1½ hours (adding more water when necessary).
8. Turn the pudding on to a serving dish and cover with hot chocolate orange sauce (page 129).
Serves 6–8.

Chocolate rice pudding

110g (4oz) short grain rice
700ml (1¼pts) milk
140ml (¼pt) single cream
55g (2oz) butter
85g (3oz) caster sugar
3 eggs
110g (4oz) plain chocolate
For serving – *single cream*

1. Butter a 1¾pt baking dish. Preheat the oven to 150°C. (300°F., gas mark 2).
2. Wash the rice thoroughly in cold water, then drain it.
3. Pour the milk and cream into a pan. Stir in the rice and bring slowly to simmering point. Leave to cook on a low heat until the rice is almost tender – about 12 minutes.
4. Add the butter and sugar. Stir until the butter has melted and the sugar dissolved. Remove from heat and leave the rice to cool for about 5 minutes.
5. Beat the eggs thoroughly. Grate the chocolate. Stir them both into the rice.
6. Pour the rice into the dish and place below the middle shelf of the oven. Bake for 35–45 minutes.
7. Serve with single cream.
Serves 4.

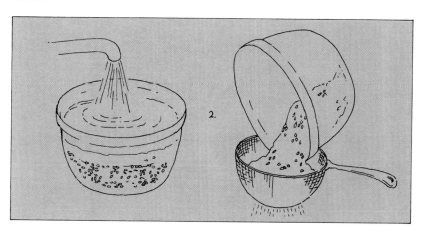

Wholesome chocolate pudding

110g (4oz) plain chocolate
55g (2oz) butter
285ml (½pt) milk
55g (2oz) soft brown sugar
2 eggs, separated
140g (5oz) wholewheat breadcrumbs
55g (2oz) raisins

1. Butter a 2pt pudding basin.
2. Melt the chocolate in the usual way (page 15). Add the butter.
3. Warm the milk then add it to the chocolate. Sprinkle the sugar into the milk and stir for 2–3 minutes. Remove from heat.
4. Lightly beat the egg yolks and add them to the mixture. Stir in half the breadcrumbs and mix thoroughly.
5. Stir in the remaining breadcrumbs and the raisins. Mix thoroughly.
6. Whisk the egg whites until stiff peaks form. Carefully fold them into the mixture.
7. Spoon the mixture into the buttered basin, cover with a double layer of greaseproof paper and secure with string.
8. Steam for 1¼ to 1½ hours, or until risen and firm to the touch, adding more water when required.
9. Turn the pudding on to a plate and serve with hot nutty chocolate sauce (page 129).
Serves 4–6.

Maltese chocolate pancakes

55g (2oz) almond flakes
55g (2oz) glacé cherries
55g (2oz) candied peel
140g (5oz) plain chocolate
390g (14oz) rikotta
85g (3oz) caster sugar

200g (7oz) plain flour
pinch of salt
15g (½oz) cocoa
2 eggs, separated
285ml (½pt) milk
55g (2oz) caster sugar
1½ teasp lemon rind, grated
clear honey

Rikotta was originally produced in Italy. The Maltese, whose cuisine has been influenced by Italy, Greece, France and England, make their rikotta with milk and (pure) sea water. Unless you travel to Malta you will be unable to obtain the true Maltese cheese: Italian rikotta will suffice, or even cottage cheese, bearing in mind that the latter has a slightly different texture and flavour.

1. Chop the almond flakes, cherries and candied peel as finely as possible. Grate the chocolate and set aside 55g (2oz). Mix the nuts, fruit and chocolate in a basin, then add the rikotta and sugar. Mix thoroughly and set to one side.
2. Sieve the flour, salt and cocoa into a basin.
3. Add the egg yolks and beat in half the milk. Whisk thoroughly, then whisk in the remaining milk.
4. Whisk the egg whites until stiff peaks form. Whisk in the sugar, a little at a time, and the lemon rind, then carefully fold this mixture into the batter.
5. Heat a little butter in a frying pan and pour in just enough batter to cover the bottom. Cook until golden brown on the under-surface. Toss the pancake, or turn it with a palette knife. Brown the other side, then turn it on to a plate. Repeat until all the batter is used, keeping the cooked pancakes hot.
6. Fill each pancake with the rikotta mixture, roll, dribble the honey along the top and sprinkle with the remaining grated chocolate.
Serves 8.

Photograph opposite.
Maltese chocolate flavoured pancakes are filled with a rich cheese confection and topped with honey and grated chocolate.

Chocolate bread and butter pudding

2 cardamom pods
425ml (¾pt) milk
45g (1½oz) caster sugar
3 eggs
4 thin slices bread
55g (2oz) butter
55g (2oz) sultanas
85g (3oz) plain chocolate
For serving – *single or whipped cream*

1. Pour the milk into a pan. Split the cardamom pods in two. Put the pods, seeds and sugar into the milk. Heat gently until boiling point is almost reached. Remove from heat and leave on one side for 5 minutes.
2. Butter the bread, then cut off the crusts. Use the remaining butter to grease a 1½pt ovenproof pie dish. Cut the slices into quarters and arrange them in the dish – a layer of bread and butter, sprinkled with sultanas, another layer sprinkled with sultanas, finishing with just bread and butter. Preheat the oven to 180°C. (350°F., gas mark 4).
3. Melt the chocolate in the usual way (page 15).
4. Beat the eggs thoroughly and stir them into the milk. Strain the milk into a wide-necked jug.
5. Stir the melted chocolate into the milk and pour carefully over the bread and butter. Bake in the centre of the oven for 40–50 minutes.
6. Serve with custard, single cream or a dollop of whipped cream.
Serves 4–6.

Chocolate feather pudding

1 egg
140g (5oz) caster sugar
225ml (8fl. oz) milk
1 tblsp butter
55g (2oz) plain chocolate
170g (6oz) plain flour
pinch of salt
1½ teasp baking powder
½ teasp vanilla essence

1. Preheat the oven to 180°C. (350°F., gas mark 4). Butter 8 ramekin dishes.
2. Beat the egg until smooth. Gradually add the sugar and beat thoroughly. Stir in the milk.
3. Melt the chocolate in the usual way (page 15). Add the butter. When both have melted mix them thoroughly, then beat into the milk mixture.
4. Sieve the flour, salt and baking powder together, then gradually stir into the milk mixture.
5. Add the vanilla essence and mix all the ingredients again thoroughly.
6. Divide the mixture between the ramekin dishes. Cover with foil and steam in the oven – place the ramekins in a baking tin of hot water – for about 30 minutes.
7. Serve immediately with chocolate caramel sauce (page 131).
Serves 8.

Chocolate omelette

55g (2oz) plain chocolate
1 tblsp water
4 eggs, separated
4 tblsp caster sugar
butter for frying

1. Melt the chocolate in the usual way (page 15), and add the tablespoon of water. Remove from heat and leave to cool.
2. Beat the egg yolks thoroughly. Mix them into the chocolate with the sugar.
3. Whisk the egg whites until soft peaks form, then fold them into the mixture.
4. Melt 2 tablespoonfuls of butter in an omelette pan, pour in the mixture and cook on a moderate heat. Stir the outer edges, with a fork, towards the centre until the omelette is cooked – it should be moist, not dry, and the egg will continue to set after being removed from the heat.
5. Serve, folded double, on a warm plate.
Serves 1–2.

Chocolate fondue

225g (8oz) plain chocolate
200g (7oz) double cream
55g (2oz) caster sugar
55g (2oz) butter
1½ tblsp Tia Maria, brandy or rum
For serving – fresh fruit pieces and sponge fingers

1. Pour the cream into a heavy-based pan on the lowest heat. Break the chocolate into small pieces and melt in the cream.
2. Stir in the sugar.
3. Chop the butter and add it to the cream. Stir continuously until the butter has melted and the sugar dissolved.
4. Stir in the liqueur, brandy or rum.
5. Pour the mixture into the fondue pot and place over heat.
6. Serve with banana sliced into thick rounds; whole fresh strawberries; cubes of pineapple (fresh or tinned); segments of orange; seedless grapes; neat slices of pineapple, pears or apples; and sponge fingers or squares of almond flavoured sponge.
Serves 6–8. See illustration on pages 102–3.

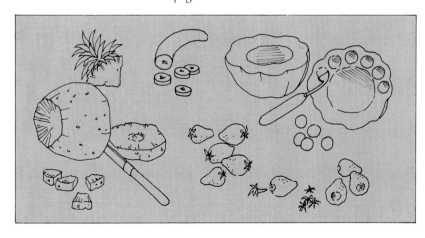

Photograph overleaf.
Try a fondue with a difference! Succulent slices of fresh fruit, or crumbly sponge fingers are dipped into a rich chocolate sauce flavoured with Tia Maria, brandy or rum.

Chocolate strudel

335g (12oz) plain flour
pinch of salt
110g (4oz) butter
1 egg
cold water to mix
1.120kg (2½lb) cooking apples
85g (3oz) caster sugar
2 teasp cinnamon
85g (3oz) sultanas
55g (2oz) cocoa
85g (3oz) chopped almonds
55g (2oz) breadcrumbs
1 tblsp icing sugar
55g (2oz) grated chocolate
double cream

1. Sieve the flour and salt together in a basin.
2. Rub half the butter into the flour until it resembles fine bread-crumbs.
3. Lightly beat the egg. Using a knife, bind the egg into the flour, adding enough water to make a sticky dough.
4. Knead to a smooth dough with well-floured hands. Cover with a cloth and set on one side for 30 minutes.
5. Meanwhile prepare the filling: peel the apples, and slice them as thinly and evenly as possible.
6. Put the sugar, cinnamon, sultanas, almonds and cocoa in a basin and mix thoroughly.
7. Spread a clean, patterned tea towel on the working surface and dust it lightly with flour.
8. Form the dough into a fat sausage. Holding one end and then the other, slap it on to the table. Do this for about 5 minutes or until bubbles appear near the surface.
9. Roll the dough on to the tea towel, and gently pull and roll until it is the same size as the tea towel.
10. Stretch the pastry until the pattern of the tea towel can be seen through it. The easiest way to stretch it is to put both hands, palms down, between the pastry and the towel, then move them up and down and sideways, keeping the oblong shape as regular as possible. Spread the stretched pastry again on to the towel.

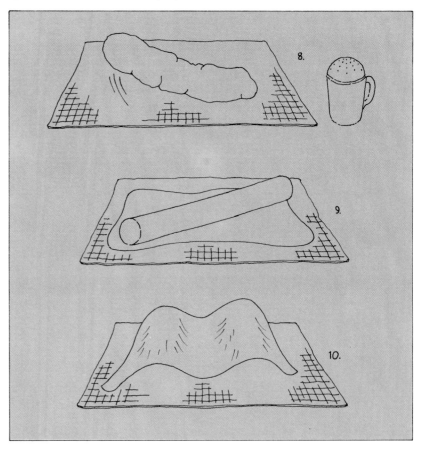

11. Melt the remaining butter (keep some back for brushing the strudel) and, when the butter is hot, fry the breadcrumbs until crisp.
12. Preheat the oven to 200°C. (400°F., gas mark 6).
13. Leaving a 25mm (1in.) border around the pastry, cover with the fried breadcrumbs, then the apple slices and finally the cocoa mixture.

14. Roll up the pastry by using the tea towel to push each roll forward.

15. Carefully place the roll, using the tea towel as support, on to a lightly buttered baking tray and form it into a horse-shoe shape. Brush with the remaining melted butter.

16. Place in the oven and bake for 10 minutes. Reduce heat to 190°C. (375°F., gas mark 5) and bake for a further 30 minutes.

17. Place on a serving dish. When the strudel is warm, dredge with icing sugar and sprinkle the chocolate on top.

18. Serve warm with a tablespoonful of whipped double cream.
Serves 6–8.

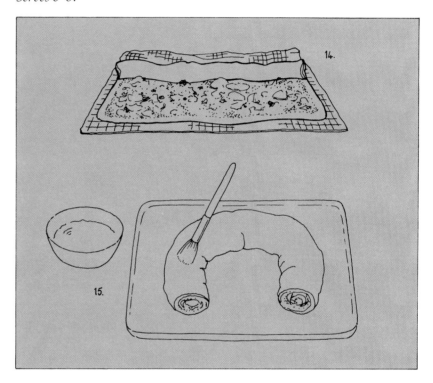

Chocolate almond soufflé

110g (4oz) plain chocolate
3 tblsp Amaretto (almond liqueur)
85g (3oz) caster sugar
4 egg yolks
6 egg whites
55g (2oz) finely chopped almonds

1. Butter a 2pt soufflé dish. Preheat the oven to 190°C. (375°F., gas mark 5).

2. Melt the chocolate in the usual way (page 15). Add the Amaretto and sugar. Remove from heat and leave to cool slightly.

3. Lightly beat the egg yolks, then beat them gradually into the mixture. Mix in the almonds.

4. Whisk the egg whites until soft peaks form. Fold them carefully into the mixture using a metal spoon.

5. Pour the mixture into the soufflé dish and place on a baking sheet in the centre of the oven. Bake for 20 minutes. The top should be crispy and the centre creamy.

6. Serve hot with soft vanilla ice cream or whipped cream.

Chocolate fruit crumble

900g (2lb) cooking apples
140g (5oz) dried apricots
1 banana (firm)
30g (1oz) demerara sugar
140g (5oz) plain chocolate

170g (6oz) wholewheat flour
55g (2oz) plain flour
55g (2oz) rolled oats
110g (4oz) butter
55g (2oz) demerara sugar
55g (2oz) finely chopped unblanched almonds
For serving – single or whipped cream

1. Peel and slice the apples. Chop the apricots. Place in a pan with 5–6 tablespoonfuls of cold water. Cook on a low heat until the apples are just tender.
2. Slice the banana into rounds. Arrange all the fruit, sprinkled with the 30g (1oz) of sugar, in a 3pt ovenproof dish.
3. Melt 85g (3oz) of the chocolate in the usual way (page 15) and pour it over the fruit. Preheat the oven to 180°C. (350°F., gas mark 4).
4. Mix the flours and oats in a basin. Chop the butter and rub it in until the mixture resembles breadcrumbs. Mix in the sugar.
5. Spoon the mixture over the fruit and chocolate. Place the dish on a high shelf and bake for 30–35 minutes.
6. Grate the remaining chocolate and mix with the almonds.
7. Leave the crumble to cool for 5 minutes, then sprinkle the chocolate and nut mixture on top.
8. Serve with single cream or a generous tablespoonful of whipped cream.
Serves 6–8.

Chocolate pecan pudding

85g (3oz) cocoa
55g (2oz) ground rice
55g (2oz) caster sugar
1 teasp baking powder
30g (1oz) butter
55g (2oz) plain chocolate
2 eggs
55g (2oz) pecans
285ml (½pt) water
85g (3oz) dark brown sugar

1. Butter a 2pt baking dish. Preheat the oven to 180°C. (350°F., gas mark 4).
2. Sift together in a basin 55g (2oz) of the cocoa and the baking powder. Stir in the ground rice and caster sugar.
3. Melt the chocolate in the usual way (page 15) and add the 30g (1oz) of butter. When both have melted, stir thoroughly and remove from heat.
4. Beat the eggs in a basin, stir in the chocolate and butter mixture, then add to the dry ingredients.
5. Chop the pecans finely and add to the mixture. Pour into the buttered dish.
6. Boil the water and leave until warm.
7. Mix the brown sugar and remaining cocoa in a basin and gradually whisk in the warm water.
8. Pour the water over the pudding.
9. Bake the pudding in the centre of the oven for 30 minutes, or until risen and firm in the centre.
This pudding comes with its own sauce.
Serves 4.

Photograph opposite.
Chocolate fruit crumble uses apples, apricots and bananas, topped with melted chocolate, as the fruit base, which is then covered with a crumble mixture sprinkled with grated chocolate and nuts.

Chocolate meringue custard

3 eggs, separated
225g (8oz) caster sugar
100g (3½oz) cocoa
110g (4oz) fresh white breadcrumbs
570ml (1pt) milk

1. Butter a 3pt oven dish. Preheat the oven to 160°C. (325°F., gas mark 3).
2. Beat the egg yolks and 55g (2oz) of the sugar until pale and fluffy. Beat in 55g (2oz) of the cocoa.
3. Heat the milk in a heavy-based pan. Do not allow to reach boiling point.
4. Whisk a little of the hot milk into the egg mixture, then pour into the milk. Stir continuously on the lowest heat until the custard begins to thicken. Remove from heat and mix the breadcrumbs thoroughly into the custard. Pour the mixture into the dish.
5. Whisk the egg whites until stiff peaks form and add half the remaining sugar. Continue beating until the whites are stiff and shiny. Fold in the remaining sugar and sift the remaining cocoa on top.
6. Whisk the mixture again, then spoon on top of the custard, moving the spoon round and up to form swirls and peaks.
7. Bake below the centre shelf for 45 minutes.
Serves 4.

Poached chocolate pears

Approx. 850ml (1½pt) water
170g (6oz) sugar
Rind of 1 orange, thinly pared
1 cinnamon stick
6 pears (firm)

100g (3½oz) plain chocolate
15g (½oz) butter
1 tblsp orange juice
2 tblsp pear syrup
For serving – chocolate ice cream

1. Put the water, sugar and orange rind into a pan. Break the cinnamon stick and add it to the water. Heat gently until the sugar dissolves.
2. Peel the pears finely, leaving the stalks. Place them in the syrup, cover with a lid and poach on a low heat for 15 minutes, or until just tender. Remove from heat and leave to cool, still covered.
3. Melt the chocolate in the usual way (page 15) and add the butter. When both have melted remove from heat.
4. Beat a tablespoonful of juice from the orange and 2 tablespoonfuls of pear syrup from the pan into the chocolate.
5. Remove the pears from the pan with a draining spoon and place them on a serving dish. Pour the sauce over each pear. Place a scoop of chocolate ice cream between each pear.
Serves 6.

Cold Desserts

Cold Desserts

Chocolate orange mousse

280g (10oz) plain chocolate
1 firm orange
2 tblsp double cream
4 eggs, separated

1. Place 12 bun cases in a deep bun tray.
2. Melt 170g (6oz) of the chocolate in the usual way (page 15).
3. Drop 1 teaspoonful of chocolate into each case and, using the back of a spoon, spread it evenly over the sides and base. Leave to set in a cool place for 45 minutes.
4. Peel away the paper cases carefully.
5. Grate the orange finely, try not to remove the pith. Put 12 strands of peel to one side. Squeeze the orange.
6. Melt the remaining chocolate, stir in 2 tblsp of the orange juice. Remove from heat and stir in the 4 egg yolks.
7. Whip the cream in a small basin, then fold it into the chocolate.
8. Whisk the egg whites until they are stiff. Very carefully add 2 tblsp at a time of the chocolate, folding it in slowly with a spatula.
9. Spoon the mixture into the chocolate cases and top each with a sliver of peel.
10. Refrigerate for 1½ hours before serving.
Serves 8–12.

Raspberry chocolate trifle

1 chocolate Swiss roll
3 tblsp sherry or framboise (raspberry liqueur)
450g (1lb) fresh or frozen raspberries
4 tblsp cornflour
2 tblsp cocoa
1 tblsp caster sugar
570ml (1pt) milk
2 egg yolks
225ml (8fl. oz) whipping cream
•55g (2oz) milk chocolate
55g (2oz) plain chocolate

1. Refrigerate the milk and the plain chocolate.
2. Slice the Swiss roll, then arrange the slices neatly over the base and sides of a glass serving dish.
3. Pour the sherry/liqueur over the sponge.
4. Place the raspberries evenly in the basin.
5. Blend the cornflour, cocoa, sugar and a little of the milk to a smooth paste, in a heavy-based pan. Add the remaining milk and bring to the boil, stirring continuously.
6. Remove from heat and beat in the egg yolks. Cook gently for 3 minutes without boiling.
7. Carefully pour the mixture over the fruit and sponge. Smooth the surface with a spatula, then leave to cool.
8. Whip the cream and spread evenly over the cold custard.
9. Grate the 2 chocolates and sprinkle liberally over the cream.
Serves 6.

Blackcurrant chocolate meringue

*4 egg whites
pinch of salt
170g (6oz) caster sugar
45g (1½oz) cocoa
110g (4oz) nibbed almonds
450g (1lb) blackcurrants, fresh, frozen or
tinned
285ml (½pt) double cream*

The meringue can be made a few days in advance and kept in an airtight container. The completed dessert should be left for a few hours before serving to prevent the meringue from splintering when cut.

1. Lightly oil and line with rice paper the base of two 200mm (8in.) sandwich tins.
2. Preheat the oven to 190°C. (375°F., gas mark 5).
3. Whisk the egg whites. Add the salt and continue whisking until soft peaks are formed. Gradually fold in the sugar.
4. Sift the cocoa over the mixture, sprinkle the nuts and carefully fold in.
5. Divide the mixture between the two tins and smooth over with a spatula. Bake for 40 minutes.
6. Remove and leave in the tins for 10 minutes. Turn on to a wire tray and leave to cool.
7. Whip the cream. Spread half on one of the meringues, then pipe a scroll with the remaining half around the edge of the other.
8. Divide the blackcurrants, placing some over the spread cream and the rest inside the scroll. Sandwich the two meringues together.
Serves 10.

The tangy taste of blackcurrants enhances the rich taste of chocolate flavoured meringue. A thick, whipped cream filling and piped scroll topping complete this delicious dessert.

Chocolate soufflé

15g (½oz) powdered gelatine
4 tblsp cold water
425ml (¾pt) milk
3 eggs, separated
55g (2oz) caster sugar
170g (6oz) milk chocolate
55g (2oz) plain chocolate
225ml (8fl. oz) double cream
8 chocolate leaves for decoration

1. Make a collar for the (1 pint) soufflé dish: secure a double sheet of greaseproof paper around the outside of the dish with string. The collar should stand 50mm (2in.) above the rim. Lightly oil the dish and inside the collar.

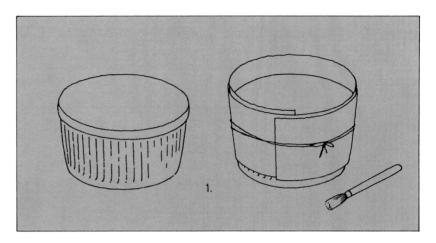

2. Sprinkle the gelatine over the water and leave to dissolve in a cup, in a pan of barely simmering water.
3. Pour the milk into a pan and bring to the boil.
4. Cream the egg yolks and sugar in a basin, then stir in the boiling milk. Return the mixture to the pan and cook gently, stirring continuously until it thickens. Remove from heat.
5. Break the milk chocolate into small pieces. Add them to the custard and stir until melted. Stir in the dissolved gelatine. Leave to cool.
6. Lightly whip half the cream and stir it into the custard.
7. Whisk the egg whites until soft peaks form, then fold into the custard using a metal spoon.
8. Turn the mixture into the prepared dish and refrigerate for 2½ hours.
9. Untie the string carefully and remove the collar: press the blade of a palette knife against the dish, move the knife around slowly while, at the same time, carefully peeling away the paper.

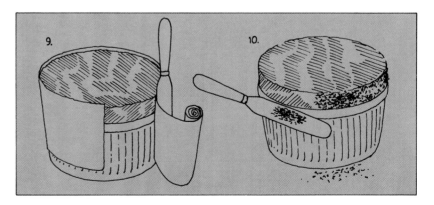

10. Whip the remaining cream. Carefully spread some around the soufflé sides. Grate the plain chocolate and, using a palette knife, flick the chocolate on to the cream.
11. Pipe stars around the top edge of the soufflé with the remaining cream, finishing with a star in the centre. Arrange the leaves coming out from the centre star.
Serves 6.

115

Chocolate ginger ice cream

4 egg yolks
110g (4oz) sugar
285ml (½pt) single cream
140g (5oz) plain chocolate
4 pieces preserved ginger
285ml (½pt) double cream
ginger syrup (see below)

For home-made ginger syrup
225g (½lb) root ginger
570ml (1pt) cold water
895g (2lb) sugar
½ stick cinnamon

1. Beat the egg yolks and sugar until thick and creamy.
2. Break the chocolate into pieces and melt it in the single cream over a low heat.
3. Slowly add the chocolate cream to the egg yolks, stirring continuously. Put the basin over a pan of simmering water and stir until the mixture thickens. Remove from heat and leave to cool.
4. Slice the ginger very finely and add it to the cooled mixture.
5. Whip the double cream lightly and fold it into the mixture. Cover with foil and place in the freezer.
6. As the mixture begins to set, make sure the ginger is evenly distributed by carefully putting a fork through it and lifting. Re-cover and freeze for 2–3 hours, or until firm.
7. Pour a tablespoonful of ginger syrup over each helping and decorate with 2 chocolate leaves. (See below for ginger syrup and page 18 for making chocolate leaves.)

Home-made ginger syrup is a useful addition to the store cupboard. As well as being the perfect complement to chocolate ice cream it can be poured over milk puddings, fruit salad, sponge puddings; added to lime jelly; or made into a tangy drink using iced water, a tablespoonful of syrup and the juice of 2 oranges.
1. Put the root ginger into a basin, cover with the cold water and leave to steep overnight.
2. Drain the ginger and slice as finely as possible.
3. Put the ginger in a heavy-based pan. Add the water, sugar and cinnamon. Stir over a low heat until the sugar has dissolved.
4. Put a lid on the pan and cook gently for an hour.
5. Strain the syrup through a piece of muslin. Leave to cool, then pour it into screw-topped bottles.
Serves 6–8.

Tutti-frutti chocolate bombe

170g (6oz) plain chocolate
285ml (½pt) milk
3 egg yolks
85g (3oz) sugar
285ml (½pt) double cream

———

425ml (¾pt) single cream
3 egg yolks
55g (2oz) caster sugar
85g (3oz) chopped dried apricots
30g (1oz) sultanas
85g (3oz) chopped glacé cherries
1 teasp chopped angelica
55g (2oz) nibbed almonds
30g (1oz) flaked almonds
30g (1oz) grated chocolate

1. Break 110g (4oz) of the chocolate into pieces and stir them into the milk, over a low heat. Do not allow the milk to boil.
2. Put the 3 egg yolks and 85g (3oz) of sugar in a basin and beat until thick and creamy. Slowly add the chocolate milk, stirring continuously.
3. Pour the mixture back into the pan, over a low heat, and stir until it thickens. Remove from heat.
4. Strain the mixture into a basin and leave to cool in the refrigerator.
5. Grate the remaining chocolate and stir it into the cooled mixture.
6. Whip the cream and fold it into the mixture. Pour into a 2½pt basin and refrigerate for an hour.
7. Put a 1½pt basin in the centre of the mixture with enough weight inside to bring the mixture level with the top of the basin. Cover with foil and freeze for 3 hours or until firm.
8. Remove weights and pour some hot water into the smaller basin. When the ice cream begins to melt, carefully remove the basin. Return the ice cream, covered, to the freezer.

9. To make the tutti-frutti ice cream, follow instructions 1 to 3, using the single cream instead of milk and omitting the chocolate.
10. Fold in the fruits and nuts and leave to cool for an hour.
11. Pour the mixture into the chocolate ice cream cavity, cover with foil and freeze for 3–4 hours or until firm.
12. To turn out the bombe, dip the basin in very hot water and invert on to a cold serving dish.
13. Decorate with the flaked almonds, grated chocolate and whipped cream if desired.
Serves 8–12.

Chocolate almond queen

170g (6oz) plain chocolate
3 tblsp Amaretto (almond liqueur)
170g (6oz) soft butter
85g (3oz) caster sugar
1 egg, separated
110g (4oz) ground almonds
45g (1½oz) milk chocolate
85ml (3fl. oz) double cream
85g (3oz) unblanched almonds

1. Lightly oil a 1¾pt round or oblong dish.
2. Melt the chocolate in the usual way (page 15) and stir in the Amaretto. Remove from heat.
3. Beat the butter and sugar until the whole is pale and fluffy. Add the egg yolk, melted chocolate and ground almonds, beating after each addition.
4. Whisk the egg white to soft peaks. Fold it into the mixture with a metal spoon.
5. Pour the mixture into the mould, cover and refrigerate for 2–3 hours, or until firm.
6. Dip the dish, up to the rim, in very hot water for a few seconds. Turn the dessert on to a chilled serving dish – hold the two together and give one sharp shake.
7. Melt the milk chocolate in the usual way (page 15). Make an icing bag (page 17), spoon the melted chocolate into it, snip the end off the bag and pipe a continuous circle around the top of the dessert. Start on the outside edge and finish with a blob in the centre. Fix 3 almonds into the blob. (If the dessert is oblong, pipe a continuous zigzag from one end to the other. Pipe a blob at each end and one in the centre. Fix 3 almonds into each blob.)
8. Whip the double cream and pipe stars around the base of the dessert. Fix 2 almonds into the top of each star.
Serves 4–6.

Chocolate orange charlotte

300g (11oz) tin tangerine segments
280g (10oz) plain chocolate
55g (2oz) granulated sugar
orange food colour
225g (8oz) butter
85g (3oz) caster sugar
3 eggs, separated
335g (12oz) double cream
2 tblsp Grand Marnier
Peel of 1 orange, finely grated
about 24 sponge fingers

1. Line a 2pt charlotte mould with greaseproof paper.
2. Drain the tangerines (keep the juice) and dry them thoroughly with paper towels.
3. Melt the chocolate in the usual way (page 15), then remove from heat.
4. Put the granulated sugar in a saucer and mix in thoroughly several drops of orange colouring. Leave on one side.
5. Arrange the sponge fingers around the sides of the charlotte mould, using a little melted chocolate to secure their position.
6. Beat the caster sugar and butter until the mixture is pale and fluffy. Add the egg yolks, one at a time. Beat thoroughly. Stir in the remaining melted chocolate, the Grand Marnier, and the grated orange peel.
7. Whisk the egg whites to soft peaks. Fold them into the mixture carefully, a little at a time.
8. Whip 225ml (8oz) of the cream lightly and gently fold it into the mixture.
9. Spoon the mixture into the mould and refrigerate overnight.
10. Turn the charlotte on to a serving dish and remove the greaseproof paper.
11. While whisking the remaining cream, add a few drops of orange colour. Pipe stars around the top and bottom edges of the charlotte.
12. Position a tangerine segment between each star around the base. Position four, like a windmill sail, on the centre top.
Serves 6–8.

Photograph opposite.
Tangerines give this Chocolate charlotte a unique flavour and Grand Marnier and the zest of orange peel enhance the taste of chocolate.
The dessert is decorated with tangerine segments and whipped cream stars piped around the top and bottom edges.

Milk chocolate jelly

3 teasp gelatine powder
455ml (16fl. oz) milk
110g (4oz) plain chocolate
55g (2oz) caster sugar
110ml (4fl. oz) double cream

1. Put 3 tablespoonfuls of hot water in a dish over a pan of simmering water. Sprinkle the gelatine in the dish and leave until it dissolves and the water becomes clear.
2. Pour the milk into a pan. Break 85g (3oz) of the chocolate into pieces and add it to the milk with the sugar. Heat gently until the chocolate has melted, the sugar dissolved and the milk is lukewarm.
3. Remove from heat and whisk in the gelatine.
4. Pour cold water into a 1¾pt jelly mould, swish it around, then shake away excess.
5. Whisk the mixture again and pour into the mould. Refrigerate for 2–3 hours, or until set.
6. Dip the mould, up to the rim, in boiling water for a second or two, then turn the jelly on to a serving dish – hold the two together and give one sharp shake.
7. Whip the cream and pipe stars or scrolls around the base of the jelly, and one star on top.
8. Grate the remaining chocolate and sprinkle it over the cream.
Serves 4–6.

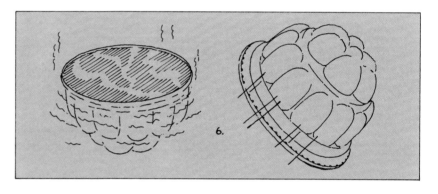

Milk chocolate jelly is topped with whipped cream and decorated with stars or scrolls around the base. Sprinkle grated chocolate over the cream for additional flavour.
You can find unusual and attractive jelly moulds in antique shops, or they can often be purchased for very little at jumble sales.

St Emilion au chocolat

450g (1lb) macaroons
5 tblsp cognac mixed with 3 tblsp water
140ml (¼pt) milk
225g (8oz) plain chocolate
110g (4oz) butter
110g (4oz) caster sugar
1 egg
2 tblsp double cream

1. Place the macaroons in a shallow dish and sprinkle them with the cognac water.
2. Bring the milk to boil, then leave to cool for about 10 minutes.
3. Melt the chocolate in the usual way (page 15).
4. Put the butter and sugar in a basin and beat until light and fluffy.
5. Add the egg to the cooled milk and mix thoroughly.
6. While the chocolate is still over the hot water, pour in the milk and beat until smooth.
7. Add this mixture to the butter, a little at a time, and beat again until very smooth.

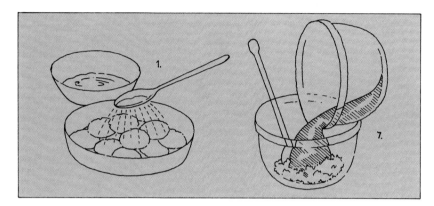

8. Refrigerate for half an hour, or until the mixture begins to thicken.
9. Line the bottom of a serving dish with macaroons. Pour in half the chocolate mixture, then position another layer of macaroons on top. Pour in the remaining mixture.
10. Drop the cream at intervals over the surface of the mixture, then swirl it in to give a marbled effect.
11. Position the remaining macaroons around the edge.
12. Refrigerate for at least 12 hours before serving.
Serves 6–8.

Chocolate cheesecake

140g (5oz) digestive biscuits
55g (2oz) plain chocolate
100g (3½oz) butter
450g (1lb) full fat soft cheese
170g (6oz) caster sugar
30g (1oz) cocoa
2 eggs
110g (4oz) milk chocolate
170ml (6fl. oz) double cream
packet of milk chocolate buttons

1. Chill a 200mm (8in.) springform cake tin.
2. Put the biscuits in a strong polythene bag and crush them with a rolling pin.
3. Melt the chocolate in the usual way (page 15). Add the butter and stir occasionally until melted. Remove from heat and mix in the biscuit crumbs.
4. Press the mixture evenly on to the base and about 50mm (2in.) up the sides of the chilled cake tin. Refrigerate.
5. Set the oven to 180°C. (350°F., gas mark 4).
6. Cream the cheese, sugar and cocoa together in a basin.
7. Add the eggs and beat the mixture until smooth. Pour into the biscuit mould. Bake in centre of oven for 25 minutes.
8. Leave to cool.
9. Melt the chocolate and remaining butter in the usual way (page 15). Remove from heat and leave to cool for 5 minutes. Pour over the cooled cheesecake and leave to set.
10. Whip the cream and pipe large stars over the surface of the chocolate. Place a chocolate button, sideways, into the top of each star.
Serves 8–10.

Spiced chocolate custards

225ml (8fl. oz) milk
2 crushed cardamom pods
1 vanilla pod
1 crushed cinnamon stick
¼ teasp freshly grated nutmeg
225g (8oz) plain chocolate
5 egg yolks
140ml (¼pt) single cream

1. Pour the milk into a pan. Add the spices, bring the milk to boiling point, then strain.
2. Break 170g (6oz) of the chocolate into pieces and add it to the milk. Place on a low heat, stirring until the chocolate has melted and blended thoroughly into the milk.
3. Add the egg yolks and beat well.
4. Continue cooking the mixture on a low heat, stirring continuously until it thickens and becomes creamy.
5. Remove from heat and stir occasionally until the custard cools.
6. Pour into 6 small ramekin dishes and swirl the cream into the surface of each custard.
7. Grate the remaining chocolate and sprinkle on top.
Serves 6.

Iced mint chocolate mousse

140g (5oz) plain chocolate
4 eggs, separated
55g (2oz) caster sugar
2 tblsp crème de menthe
140ml (¼pt) double cream
crushed clear mints and
chocolate leaves to decorate

1. Melt the chocolate in the usual way (page 15).
2. Beat the egg yolks and sugar until the mixture is fluffy and pale.
3. Beat the melted chocolate into the eggs, then stir in the crème de menthe.
4. Lightly whip the cream and fold it into the mixture.
5. Whisk the egg whites until they are stiff, then fold into the mixture.
6. Pour into glass or ramekin dishes and freeze.
7. Serve straight from the freezer. Decorate with half a teaspoonful of crushed clear mints, and 2 chocolate leaves, per serving. (See page 18 for how to make chocolate leaves.)
Serves 6–8.

Photograph opposite.
Iced mint chocolate mousse is a light and fluffy dessert. It is flavoured with crème de menthe and decorated with crushed clear mints.

Chocolate meringue pie

110g (4oz) plain flour
¼ teasp salt
55g (2oz) butter
cold water to mix

30g (1oz) cornflour
55g (2oz) cocoa
285ml (½pt) milk
85g (3oz) sugar
15g (½oz) butter
2 large eggs, separated
110g (4oz) caster sugar
55g (2oz) plain chocolate

1. Sieve the flour and salt together in a basin. Cut the butter into thin slices and, using cold fingertips, rub it lightly into the flour until it resembles fine breadcrumbs.
2. Add a few drops of water at a time to the mixture and bind it together with a knife. The mixture should become one lump, leaving the sides of the basin perfectly clean.
3. Refrigerate the pastry, on a lightly floured plate, for 15 minutes. Pre-heat the oven to 210°C. (425°F., gas mark 7).
4. Roll out the pastry and line a 180mm (7in.) flan tin. Flute the edges and prick the base with a fork.
5. Cut a piece of greaseproof paper, slightly larger than the flan tin, butter it lightly and position it (buttered side down) over the pastry. Scatter dried beans, peas or rice over the paper.
6. Bake for 15 minutes, then remove and leave to cool. Reduce oven temperature to 180°C. (350°F., gas mark 4).
7. Blend the cornflour and cocoa with a little of the milk.
8. Heat the remaining milk, pour it into the cocoa mixture, return it to the pan and heat gently for 2–3 minutes, stirring continuously. Remove from heat.
9. Lightly beat the egg yolks. Stir them into the mixture with the sugar and butter. Mix well and pour into the pastry case (having first removed the beans and paper).
10. Bake in the centre of the oven for 20 minutes. Reduce the oven temperature to 150°C. (300°F., gas mark 2).
11. Whisk the egg whites until stiff. Add half the sugar and whisk until stiff again. Carefully fold in the remaining sugar, then spoon the meringue over the cooked chocolate, putting it into small peaks.
12. Bake on the lowest shelf for 30–35 minutes, or until the meringue is lightly coloured and crisp to the touch. Leave to cool.
13. Melt the chocolate in the usual way (page 15). Make an icing bag (see page 17), spoon in the melted chocolate, snip the end off the bag and drizzle the chocolate all over the meringue.
Serves 4–6.

Chocolate and meringue nut sundae

55g (2oz) plain chocolate
15g (½oz) butter
1 tblsp milk
1 teasp vanilla essence
2 tblsp coffee liqueur
4 scoops vanilla ice cream
225ml (8fl. oz) double cream whipped
2 meringues, crushed
Chopped whole hazelnuts for decoration
4 sundae glasses

1. Melt the chocolate and butter in a basin over simmering hot water.
2. Stir in the milk, vanilla essence and the liqueur to make a rich, smooth sauce.
3. Put a scoop of ice cream in each of the four sundae glasses, and top it with some crushed meringue.
4. Pour a little of the sauce over it, top with a large whirl of whipped cream, and sprinkle with chopped nuts.
Serves 4.

Sauces

Sauces

Basic chocolate sauce

30g (1oz) butter
140g (5oz) bitter chocolate
30g (1oz) plain flour
285ml (½pt) cold water

1. Melt the butter and chocolate in a deep saucepan.
2. Remove from heat and stir in the flour.
3. Gradually add the water.
4. Return to heat and bring to a gentle simmer, stirring constantly, and allow to cook for approximately 5 minutes.
5. Add your own variations such as chopped nuts, liqueur, candied peel, etc.
Serve hot.

Chocolate orange sauce

1 large orange
45g (1½oz) butter
3 teasp plain flour
55g (2oz) caster sugar
1 egg, separated
55g (2oz) plain chocolate, grated

This sauce can be served with Chocolate orange pudding, on page 97.
1. Grate the orange as finely as possible, trying not to include any pith.
2. Cream the butter, then mix in the orange peel.
3. Mix the flour and sugar together and beat them into the butter. Mix in the egg yolk.
4. Extract the juice from the orange, then add enough water to make 170ml (6fl. oz). Beat this into the mixture. Add the grated chocolate.
5. Whisk the egg white until stiff peaks form.
6. Pour the mixture (not the egg whites) into a heavy-based pan and cook on the lowest heat, stirring continuously, until the mixture thickens. Remove from heat.
7. Carefully fold in the egg white and serve immediately.

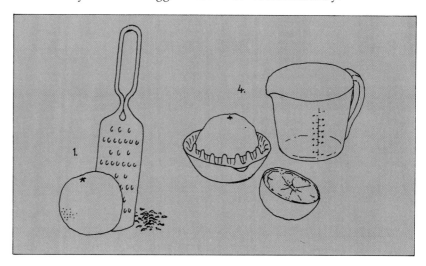

Nutty chocolate sauce

85g (3oz) plain chocolate
285ml (½pt) water
1 tblsp cornflour
55g (2oz) caster sugar
30g (1oz) butter
55g (2oz) finely chopped hazelnuts

This sauce can be served with the Wholesome chocolate pudding, on page 98.
1. Pour the water into a heavy-based pan. Break the chocolate into pieces and add it to the water. Bring to the boil.
2. Mix the cornflour to a paste with a little water, and stir it into the pan.
3. Stir in the sugar and continue stirring until the mixture thickens. Cook for a few minutes longer, stirring continuously.
4. Remove from heat and stir in the butter, then the hazelnuts.
5. Pour over the whole pudding, or serve each portion from a sauce boat.

Thick chocolate honey sauce makes an ideal accompaniment to a plain sponge pudding. It looks most decorative spooned on top of a fresh fruit salad served in a tall glass.

Chocolate mint sauce

170g (6oz) plain chocolate
140ml (¼pt) water
55g (2oz) caster sugar
1½ tblsp golden syrup
30g (1oz) butter
Few drops of peppermint essence or
2 tblsp crème de menthe

1. Grate the chocolate.
2. Pour the water into a heavy-based pan, on a low heat. Add the sugar and stir until it dissolves.
3. Stir in the golden syrup and butter. When the butter has melted bring the mixture to boil.
4. Reduce heat and simmer for 3 minutes.
5. Remove from heat and whisk in the grated chocolate.
6. Stir in the peppermint essence or crème de menthe.
Serve warm or cold over ice cream.

Spiced chocolate sauce

110g (4oz) butter
85g (3oz) caster sugar
1 tblsp dark rum
85g (3oz) plain chocolate
generous pinch each of cinnamon,
nutmeg and allspice
140ml (¼pt) double cream

1. Chop the butter into a heavy-based pan, on a low heat.
2. Stir in the sugar and rum.
3. Break the chocolate into pieces and add it to the pan.
4. Add the spices and mix thoroughly.
5. Add the cream and bring to the boil. Allow to simmer very gently for about 5 minutes.
Serve hot or cold.

Mocha sauce

55g (2oz) cocoa
140ml (¼pt) strong black coffee
85g (3oz) mild honey
85ml (3fl. oz) double cream

1. Pour the coffee into a heavy-based pan, on a low heat.
2. Sprinkle the cocoa over the coffee and mix until blended.
3. Add the honey, and mix until dissolved.
4. Whip the cream and fold it into the mixture.
5. Stirring continuously, cook the sauce until it is smooth and slightly thickened.
Serve over cream puffs, sponge pudding or ice cream.

Chocolate caramel sauce

225ml (8fl. oz) single cream
110g (4oz) plain chocolate
170g (6oz) soft brown sugar
1 tblsp butter
1 teasp vanilla essence

This sauce can be served with Chocolate feather pudding on page 100.
1. Pour the cream into a heavy-based pan, on the lowest heat.
2. Break the chocolate into pieces and add it to the cream.
3. Stir in the sugar, then the butter.
4. Continue stirring until all the ingredients are melted, dissolved and thoroughly blended.
5. Remove from heat and stir in the vanilla essence.

Chocolate ginger fudge sauce

110ml (4fl. oz) milk
2 tblsp single cream
30g (1oz) caster sugar
55g (2oz) butter
2–3 tblsp ginger syrup (page 116)
110g (4oz) plain chocolate

1. Pour the milk and cream into a heavy-based pan, on a low heat.
2. Chop the butter and add it to the pan. Add the sugar. Stir until the butter has melted and the sugar dissolved.
3. Stir in the ginger syrup. Remove from heat.
4. Break the chocolate into pieces, add it to the mixture, and stir until it is melted.
5. Return to heat and boil rapidly for 2 minutes.
Serve hot over sponge pudding or block ice cream.

Chocolate honey sauce

55g (2oz) plain chocolate
55g (2oz) granulated sugar
1 level tblsp cornflour
5 tblsp clear honey
170ml (6fl. oz) milk
55g (2oz) butter

1. Grate the chocolate and mix it with the cornflour.
2. Pour the milk into a heavy-based pan, on a low heat. Stir in the honey and sugar.
3. Gradually add the chocolate and cornflour mixture, stirring continuously, until the sauce thickens.
4. Chop the butter and add it to the pan.
5. Continue to cook slowly, until the butter melts and all the ingredients are thoroughly blended.
Serve over sponge, poached fruit or fresh fruit salad.

Chocolate coconut sauce

285ml (½pt) water
170g (6oz) granulated sugar
¼ fresh coconut
140g (5oz) milk chocolate

1. Pour the water into a heavy-based pan, on a low heat. Add the sugar and stir until it dissolves.
2. Increase heat and boil until the mixture becomes a thick syrup. Reduce heat.
3. Grate the coconut and add it to the mixture. Cook gently for about 25 minutes, or until it becomes translucent. Remove from heat.
4. Break the chocolate into pieces and stir into the mixture. Blend thoroughly.
Serve over fruit or sponge pudding, or coconut ice cream.

Chocolate almond sauce

85g (3oz) butter
70g (2½oz) plain chocolate
55g (2oz) granulated sugar
140ml (¼pt) single cream
45g (1½oz) finely chopped almonds
1 tblsp Amaretto (almond liqueur)

1. Chop the butter into a heavy-based pan, on a low heat.
2. Break the chocolate and add it to the butter. Stir in the sugar.
3. Pour in the cream. Stir continuously until the chocolate and butter have melted and the sugar dissolved. Bring to the boil, and boil for one minute. Reduce heat and stir continuously until the mixture becomes smooth and thick. Remove from heat.
4. Stir in the chopped almonds and Amaretto.
Serve hot.

Chocolate pineapple juice sauce

170g (6oz) plain chocolate
55g (2oz) butter
1 tblsp brandy
55g (2oz) soft brown sugar
1 tblsp lemon juice
3 tblsp pineapple juice

1. Break the chocolate into small pieces, and place them in a deep saucepan.
2. Add the butter, brandy, sugar, lemon juice, and pineapple juice, and heat gently until the chocolate has melted.
3. Stirring continuously, bring the sauce to a gentle boil, and simmer for 2 minutes.
Serve hot or cold.

Chocolate syrup sauce

170g (6oz) plain chocolate
3 tblsp golden syrup
225ml (8fl. oz) single cream

1. Pour the syrup into a heavy-based pan, on the lowest heat.
2. Break the chocolate into pieces and add it to the syrup. Stir well until combined.
3. Remove from heat and gradually pour in the cream, stirring continuously. Serve over sponge pudding or ice cream.

Drinks

Drinks

Traditional cocoa

4 tblsp cocoa
55g (2oz) sugar
700ml (1¼pt) gold top milk
Grated nutmeg

1. Put the cocoa and sugar in a saucepan. Cream to a smooth paste with a little of the milk.
2. Gradually stir in the remaining milk.
3. Put the pan on a medium heat and cook to very hot, but not boiling.
4. Remove from heat and whisk until frothy.
5. Quickly pour into 4 cups and grate a little nutmeg over each.
Serves 4.

Drinking chocolate

4 sticks cinnamon
55g (2oz) plain chocolate
3 tblsp water
570ml (1pt) milk
140ml (¼pt) single cream
55g (2oz) sugar
1 vanilla pod

1. Place a stick of cinnamon in each of 4 cups.
2. Break the chocolate into a pan with the water. Put on a low heat until the chocolate has melted. Allow the mixture to boil and foam, then quickly lift from heat.
3. Pour the milk into another pan, stir in the cream and add the vanilla pod. Scald – i.e. cook on a medium heat until little bubbles form round the edge of the pan. Remove the vanilla pod.
4. Pour the milk over the chocolate and whisk it.
5. Pour the chocolate into the cups and stir with the sticks of cinnamon.
Serves 4.

A selection of ingredients used in the recipes contained in this book. The tang of lemons and oranges complements the taste of chocolate, while cream and liqueurs enhance the smooth, rich flavour. Nuts and grated chocolate add the final decorative touches to any confection.

French chocolate

55g (2oz) plain chocolate
45g (1½oz) sugar
2 tblsp water
225g (8fl. oz) double cream
340ml (12fl. oz) milk

1. Pour the water into a heavy-based pan. Break the chocolate into pieces and add it to the water. Place on a low heat until the chocolate melts. Remove from heat, whisk thoroughly, and refrigerate until cold.
2. Beat the cream and blend it into the chocolate. Beat until thick. Chill again in the refrigerator.
3. To serve, divide the mixture equally between 4 cups. Heat the milk to almost boiling and pour over the chocolate cream. Stir lightly.
Serves 4.

Yoghurt and honey chocolate

55g (2oz) plain chocolate
1½ tblsp clear honey
2 tblsp water
140ml (5fl. oz) carton soft plain yoghurt
425ml (¾pt) milk
2 tblsp single cream

1. Break the chocolate into pieces and place in a pan, on a low heat with the honey and water.
2. Stir until the chocolate melts and the mixture is smooth.
3. Put the yoghurt into a basin, beat until smooth, then gradually add the milk and cream.
4. Pour the milk slowly into the chocolate, whisking gently.
5. Cook until the mixture is just about to boil. Pour it into 4 cups.
Serves 4.

Chocolate eggnog

55g (2oz) plain chocolate
700ml (1¼) milk
3 eggs
55g–85g (2oz–3oz) sugar
1 orange or lemon
Tot of rum or brandy
4 tblsp cracked ice

1. Melt the chocolate in the usual way (page 15). When melted remove from heat and gradually whisk in the milk.
2. Beat the eggs thoroughly, then add them to the milk.
3. Grate the orange or lemon finely, taking care not to remove the pith. Extract the juice and add it to the milk with the rind.
4. Add the spirit and whisk all the ingredients until thoroughly blended. Chill.
5. Place a tablespoonful of cracked ice in the bottom of 4 glasses and pour in the eggnog.
Serves 4.

Hot whisky chocolate

570ml (1pt) gold top milk
55g (2oz) plain chocolate
3 tblsp whisky
140ml (¼pt) double cream
Ground cinnamon

1. Pour the milk into a heavy-based pan. Break the chocolate into pieces and add to the milk.
2. Cook on a gentle heat until the chocolate melts, then bring to boiling point on a medium heat.
3. Beat the cream until it is stiff.
4. Remove milk from heat and add the whisky. Blend thoroughly,
5. Pour the chocolate milk into 4 cups or heat resistant glasses. Top with the cream and a sprinkling of cinnamon.
Serves 4.

Iced Brazilian chocolate

55g (2oz) plain chocolate
55g (2oz) sugar
140ml (¼pt) boiling water
285ml (½pt) milk
140ml (¼pt) single cream
225ml (8fl. oz) freshly made ground coffee
½ teasp vanilla essence
¼ teasp grated nutmeg
4 tblsp crushed ice
4 tblsp whipped cream

1. Break 45g (1½oz) of the chocolate and place in a pan with the sugar and water. Put on a low heat until the chocolate melts and the sugar dissolves.
2. Grate the remaining chocolate and leave on one side.
3. Pour the milk, cream and coffee into the chocolate and scald – i.e. cook on a medium heat until little bubbles form round the edge of the pan.
4. Add the vanilla essence and grated nutmeg.
5. Remove from heat, and whisk. Pour into a jug and refrigerate.
6. Put a tablespoonful of crushed ice in the bottom of 4 glasses. Pour in the chilled chocolate drink. Spoon the whipped cream on top and sprinkle with the grated chocolate.
Serves 4.

Mint chocolate milk shake

55g (2oz) plain chocolate
6 tblsp chocolate ice cream
285ml (½pt) chilled gold top milk
¼ teasp peppermint essence

1. Melt the chocolate in the usual way (page 15).
2. Beat the ice cream in a chilled basin and gradually add the chilled milk.
3. Beat in the melted chocolate and peppermint essence.
4. Whisk until frothy, then pour into two glasses. Serve immediately.
Serves 2.

Spiced chocolate

425ml (¾pt) milk
140ml (¼pt) double cream
1 cardamom pod
¼ teasp each ground cinnamon and nutmeg
pinch of allspice
55g (2oz) plain chocolate
55ml (2fl. oz) water
1 small egg yolk

1. Pour the milk and cream into a heavy-based pan. Bring to the boil then simmer on the lowest heat.
2. Add the cardamom pod and stir in the cinnamon, nutmeg and allspice.
3. Continue to cook on the lowest heat for 15 minutes.
4. Melt the chocolate in the usual way (page 15). Add the 55ml (2fl. oz) of water.
5. When the chocolate has melted, remove it from heat and beat in the egg yolk.
6. Add the chocolate mixture to the milk. Stir continuously until the mixture begins to thicken.
7. Pour into 4 small cups and serve at once.
Serves 4.

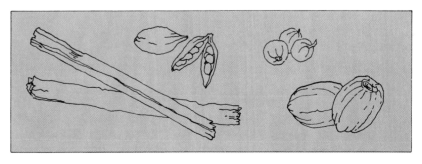

Mocha punch

1.7lt (3pt) freshly made ground coffee
570ml (1pt) double cream
2.28lt (4pt) chocolate ice cream
55ml (2fl. oz) Amaretto (almond liqueur)
85g (3oz) milk chocolate, grated

1. Prepare, then thoroughly chill, the freshly made coffee.
2. Whip the cream.
3. Pour the chilled coffee into a large chilled bowl. Beat in half the ice cream. Add the Amaretto.
4. Fold in the remaining ice cream and 340ml (12fl. oz) of the cream. Beat until smooth.
5. Pour the punch into tall glasses. Garnish with the reserved cream and a sprinkling of grated chocolate.
Serves approx. 15–20.

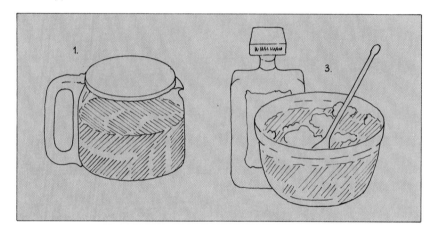

Chocolate and honey flip

1 egg
1 teasp clear honey
2 teasp cocoa powder
1 tablsp sweet sherry
285ml (½pt) milk, warmed
grated chocolate for decoration

1. Blend the egg, honey, cocoa and sherry.
2. Gradually add the warmed milk.
3. Return the mixture to the heat. Warm, but do not boil.
4. Serve at once with the grated chocolate.
Serves 2.

Index

Note. Since chocolate is common to all the recipes in this book, the word has generally been omitted from this index. Hence the recipe entitled 'Chocolate fruit crumble' will be found here under 'Fruit crumble'; and 'Chocolate almond sauce' as 'Almond sauce'; and where 'Eclairs' or 'Hot whisky' or 'Orange cake' are mentioned, the reference is, of course, to 'Chocolate eclairs', 'Hot chocolate whisky' and 'Orange chocolate cake'.

    The recipes are listed in Roman type; the section of general advice on technique and procedure are indexed in italics, e.g. 'Cooking with chocolate'.

OTHER COOKERY TITLES

DECORATING CAKES FOR CHILDREN'S PARTIES
by Polly Pinder

Thirty one cakes tastefully illustrated in full colour plus 424 step-by-step drawings that will inspire the reader to make these stunning and delightful cakes. Cake ideas include Humpty Dumpty, Superman, Winnie-the-Pooh, Fast-food addict.

Cased and paperback

DECORATING CAKES FOR SPECIAL OCCASIONS
by Polly Pinder

Filled with terrific ideas for celebration cakes. Beautifully illustrated with step-by-step drawings and colour photographs, there are 28 cake ideas including birthday cakes for the compulsive knitter and lazy gardener, and anniversaries, engagements and retirements.

Cased and paperback

HOME-MADE, and at a fraction of the cost
by Polly Pinder

This book is an amalgamation of the Home-Made paperback series. Polly Pinder's tasteful collection of money-saving delights is both imaginative and practical. She combines the exotic with the traditional and presents a colourful selection of recipes for breads, soft cheeses, pickles and chutneys, sweets and candies and natural health-giving drinks. She also gives recipes for scents and fragrances, cosmetics and soaps.

Cased and paperback

HOME MADE SERIES
by Polly Pinder

A series of paperbacks featuring many practical and money-saving ideas for making items at home. Polly Pinder and Richard Pinney guide the reader painlessly through a host of original recipes with full instructions and colour illustrations. Subjects include *Herbs in Pots, Smoked Foods, Breads* and *Drinks*

Paperback

DELICIOUS HOME-MADE CHOCOLATES
by Patrick Dalison & David Cotrez

Based on recipes taken from the famous Maison Bourdaloue in Paris, this book covers the techniques of chocolate making, followed by ten mouth-watering, illustrated recipes, including cherries in Kirsch, whisky clusters and chocolate coated fruits.

Paperback

DELICIOUS HOME-MADE PETITS FOURS
by Jean Montagard and Christiane Neuville

Originally published in France, this book describes and illustrates, with nineteen recipes, how to save money by making such delicacies as Chantilly sponge cakes, choux pastries and chocolate ganache.

Paperback

If you are interested in any of the above books or any of the art and craft titles published by Search Press send for free catalogue to
Search Press Ltd., Dept B, Wellwood, North Farm Road, Tunbridge Wells, Kent. TN2 3DR.